"*A Mother's Worst Nightmare* is a powerful story of a mother's loss and her journey to find peace. With tears in my eyes, I am riveted by the strength, resilience, and grace Dora possesses. A must read for all, it puts life into perspective."

- *Alexa Servodidio*, host of *The Alexa Radio Show - Finding Your Peace Within the Chaos*

"Near the beginning of her story the author Jean Dansak writes: '*Before I lost you though, Mom, you lost me.*' This is a heart-rending tale of what Alzheimer's does to a person's mind, and how it affects them and the people who love and care for them. In her gentle, moving way, Ms. Dansak tells of the love and admiration she always felt for her mother and the pain of witnessing her decline. Sentences like 'You never again called me by my name' jump out of the page. Despite recognizing the sadness and loss it is also a story of hope and strength. This is a beautiful story – and a tribute shared with the generosity of spirit that Ms. Dansak learnt from her mother."

- *Jenny Clift*, Author of "*The Music Inside: Tap, Change & Create a Fulfilling Career*"

"Jen's honest and heart felt explanation of her life's journey and spiritual awakening really resonated with me. Like Jen, I was teased for being a "sensitive and anxious" child and then adult. I had no idea that it was a gift and that gift had a name, "Empath". Thank You Jen for your bravery and ability to share your experiences with us! Your story inspires me to live my best and authentic life."

- *Gabriella DeCicco*, BSN,RN, Reiki Master, Intuitive and Medium

"Julie Shackelford's '*Ask and It is Given*' is a treat for Christian women and spiritual initiative's alike. Most short stories written in this genre are mostly smoke and mirrors. They give the woo-woo without shedding light on the way, the preaching without the practice. But Julie's transformative testimony rises to the challenge with great skill in this accomplished, transformative and moving short story."

- *Nikisha Ware*, Healer, Money Mindset Coach

Praise for *The Path of Awakening*

"*Why Not Me?* by Stanley E. Allen is a story of the path to wholeness and healing. You learn how he built a life of love and service by turning pain and abandonment into compassion and resilience. The joy and hope this story brings for our youth today feels so important. We MUST ensure that every 'Stanley' knows love and has the opportunity, through God, through us, to reach his/her life purpose. As we look upon our society, find the truthful, the helpful, the loving and you will find your way. I am so grateful for Mr. Allen's willingness to lift us all up with his life."

- Elizabeth Carey, President and CEO, Starr Commonwealth

"*Childhood Gifts* gently stirred memories of my own early traumas. The author shares an important message that deep childhood wounds can be carried unwittingly into adulthood, yet she manages to spare the reader any disturbing or triggering details. In the end, Hahnlen leaves us with inspiration and a sense of urgency to become the architects of our own lives. It's a loving kick in the pants to start building today, without delay."

- Denise VanBriggle, Writer, Reiki Master

"After reading *When God Shows Up* I realized that my own experiences mirror the author's in many ways. Even though we share different religions and backgrounds our understanding of God and his love are the same. We both choose to surround ourselves with people who believe this as well. As I read Maureen's experience and how she used God's love and support to find herself again after a painful divorce, I realized that God is the one true constant in our lives. The chapter touched me and reminded me of what is important in life and how we can survive to become better human beings through God. An important lesson to be learned."

- Joan Papkin

The Path of Awakening

Awakening
A Healing Journey

The exploration of Self is inextricably interwoven with the unfolding of one's life. The natural ups and downs of life can either generate personal growth or create personal fears.

~ Michael Singer, *The Untethered Soul*

The Path of Awakening - A Healing Journey

First published by Powerful Potential and Purpose Publishing 2020

Copyright © 2020 by Gloria Coppola
Cover and interior design copyright © 2020 by Candy Lyn Thomen

First printing, May 2020

Cover art, graphics and book design by Candy Lyn Thomen
Cover background photograph by msandersmusic from Pixabay

ISBN: 978-1-7349655-0-6
ISBN: 978-1-7349655-1-3 (eBook)

Published in USA

Powerful
Potential and Purpose

PUBLISHING

www.PPP-Publishing.com
Wilmington, NC

Thank you God, for the inspiration and ideas to gather and create the insights that will help others gain faith and hope in any time of crisis. I am blessed and grateful for the gifts you continue to provide me.

~Gloria Coppola, Publisher

Contents

Foreword

Invest Your Faith
in Healing

No matter where you are in your journey, you need to look at one of the most important factors in achieving a dream, maintaining a desire, or surpassing a goal; this is where you are placing your faith. What you may not have realized is that faith is actually a currency, an object of energy that we put into the flow in order to get what we want. Faith is the aggregate of what we think, say, do, and believe, as well as the unconscious competencies of our quantum memory, our DNA. This is the DNA that we can activate, our frequency, which is the actual energy we carry within ourselves. Some call it our being and essence.

For those who say that this is too "woo-woo," there is a more pragmatic example that I use. Your faith is exactly like the limit on a credit card that you can use on any online shopping platform. The more faith you have in your healing journey, the faster and more accurately you get what you want. Just like having a credit card with no credit limit, placing your faith in healing and hope is essential in order to make your dreams appear at your doorstep as rapidly as possible.

The first step in manifesting your path to awakening comes from consciously thinking about your "what," the one thing that is driving your forward in your life. Most people already know their "why," which is meant to help strengthen our connection to what inspires us, but they don't think about their "what." You need to place your hope and trust into the belief that achieving your "what" is a possibility, and then think about what you want using your foundational values.

When analyzing your foundational values, look at your personal values, your experience values, your giving values, and receiving values. Your personal values are the most valuable of your assets, the core values which you choose to prioritize in your life. The sum total of your experience and knowledge is what makes up your experience values. Many of us prioritize giving in our lives, but also feel a sense of unworthiness that prevents us from truly asking the Universe for what we want in life.

Understand that there are certain guideposts we must follow in order to effectuate what we want. Envisioning what you want with clarity means that you are placing an intention on your desires. Then, you balance that intention with the foundational values previously mentioned. When our attention and intentions are clearly and directly focused on our goal of awakening, this will bring us confidence and shift our energy, creating certainty in your journey. The moment you do that, healing becomes not a possibility, but a probability. And when you take action with consistency, meaning you do something every day, and persistence, meaning without quitting, the probabilities you create for yourself are manifested in your reality.

Too often, though, we put our faith in the things that we don't want. We vote for what we don't want and then we end up getting exactly what we don't want. In other words, what we resist persists. It's like driving a race car and focusing on the wall, then wondering why you hit the wall every time. Or, even worse, we put our faith in what other people want for us, and not only do we manifest what other people want for us, but we end up resenting them for that, feeding the needs of our ego.

When it comes to investing your faith, there is one value you should prioritize above all others. Know that there's no better place to put your faith than in the power of truth or gratitude. Gratitude is essential to clear your connection to light, love, and lessons. We're all connected to gratitude because it is what shapes our perspective of the world around us. It makes our past unbelievable, our present even better, and our future even brighter. Having gratitude allows us to be thankful for every situation that arises in our life. No matter what happens, it allows us to smile through the struggles. We also need to treat gratitude like a muscle – practice, practice, practice. We need to practice it every day, by saying "thank you" before we go to bed and saying "thank you" when we wake up. If you can manage to say "thank you" for thirty straight days, I guarantee it'll change your life. I've been blessed to be around the biggest thought leaders in the world and the universal thing that everyone agrees on is that a perspective of gratitude will change your life, no matter where you are in your journey of awakening.

Having studied physics, quantum physics, and metaphysics, it is clear to me that gratitude is the most powerful light, love, and blessing of all. Gratitude will help center you when times are tough and empower you to realize that if you can look up, you can get up. Using faith and gratitude as two tools to heal are the most efficient, effective, and statistically successful ways to be happy. Once you understand that, you will never let the "credit limit" of your faith stop you from turning your possibilities into probabilities, and you will manifest every desire you have to be happy, healthy, and thrive as you make gratitude your perspective or reality.

David Meltzer

Speaker, Author, Entrepreneur

David Meltzer is the co-founder of Sports 1 Marketing and formerly served as CEO of the renowned Leigh Steinberg Sports & Entertainment agency, which was the inspiration for the movie Jerry Maguire. He is a three-time international bestselling author, Top 100 business coach and has been recognized by Variety Magazine as their Sports Humanitarian of the Year and awarded the Ellis Island Medal of Honor.

David is one of The World's Greatest Motivator executive producers, along with Kitchen – Hamilton Productions. "Transcending Borders, Inspiring BIG Dreams!" is a platform to showcase master motivators in business success and personal development.

His life's mission is to empower OVER 1 BILLION people to be happy! This simple yet powerful mission has led him on an incredible journey to provide one thing...VALUE. In all his content and communication that's exactly what you'll receive.

His favorite piece of life changing advice is "Take action with a 'can-do-it attitude.'" He says, "Can I do it now? 100% of these things I can get done now. It helps me stay present and in the moment, and inspire others. If you can't do it now, put it into a folder and schedule time to prioritize what is most important first. It helps you stay present and it will help others too."

David's books are:

Game-Time Decision Making: High-Scoring Business Strategies from the Biggest Names in Sports

Be Unstoppable: How to Create the Life You Love

Compassionate Capitalism: A Journey to the Soul of Business

Connected To Goodness: Manifest Everything You Desire In Business And In Life

www.dmeltzer.com
www.instagram.com/davidmeltzer/
www.linkedin.com/in/davidmeltzer2/

Daydreams

We travel through life

On daydreams

To destinations far away...

Experiences unknown...

Imaginations untapped...

Follow where your mind

Takes you.

For once there,

Anything is possible

And every journey is

An Inspiration to the soul

To make the dream

Real.

- unknown

Introduction

Do we ever fully awaken on this earth?

Gloria Coppola
Publisher, Author, Spiritual Coach

"You are freedom, it's written all over you." These were the words she spoke to me in her final days of her life, still echoing through my mind decades later.

Was she part of the journey that would lead me to explore higher consciousness levels? Was I being implanted with a transmission of energy that would one day allow me to realize I am equipped with tools, urging me to shift the collective consciousness? I do believe this to be the truth now.

I was about to meet an amazing woman by chance; I dare say, no coincidence but synchronicity? Absolutely! Would she like me at first? Hell no!

It was at a time when I was re-evaluating my own spiritual truth, when a light was cast upon me. I had just come out of a dark night of the soul crisis in life where I was shown how to listen to my soul more astutely. I was forced, in essence, to stop and learn how to determine my response to life. It had brought me down to my knees. I could have reacted angrily and given up completely; however, I was guided to learn how to respond and see where my path was taking me. It took me to a dream place.

I was living on the island of Kauai, remotely situated far in the Pacific Ocean, thousands of miles from the life I once lived. It is appropriately named the Garden Isle with its magical rainforests, hundreds of waterfalls, sacred sites I would be shown and bold, beautiful rainbows. Even the stones had wisdom that would speak to me.

It all began one beautiful morning with delicious blue skies and a gentle breeze caressing my face. I was strolling in my flip-flops at the quaint plaza in downtown Hanalei appreciating another glorious moment in life and grateful to be here. As I walked into a shop, a woman name Carol, whom I barely knew, exclaimed, "You are my angel! I prayed for you to show up today." She reached out to me with a big smile and embraced me with a hug. Then she told me her mother-in-law had terminal cancer and had only been given three months to live. I often wondered how those time lines were determined and who decides this fate? After a brief conversation with Carol, she said "I knew you were the one who could help!" I found myself saying yes to caretaking her mother-in-law, Sylvie. Carol and her husband needed an occasional break. Mind you, I had never done anything like this prior, yet I felt self-assured this calling was divinely aligned for both of us.

Sylvie was about to teach me more than I could imagine. Even as I put together all these words here for you, she led me to every piece of insight, including an old journal I had misplaced for years. She was always sharing great stories and one of her conversations with a palm tree triggered this story I'm sharing with you. You see, she was a practicing avatar who was spiraling in her own human existence, confused and frustrated. An avatar is trained to have a natural ability to create and dis-create beliefs and restructure life according to a blueprint they determine. It was no wonder this feisty 80-year-old was so damned angry and pissed off. "How could I have created this cancer?" she once muttered to me. It didn't make sense.

Sylvie was born in Europe and raised Catholic, a religion which she denounced once she chose a spiritual journey. During my time with her I witnessed the depths of healing beyond what we conceive. Her process became one in which she would resolve her own relationship with Jesus, just before she chose to transition in her life. It was a necessary discovery of her own unconscious beliefs that was holding her back.

The day I walked into her home, I can still remember the floor boards creaking as she just stared at me, making me feel very uncomfortable. This cranky woman didn't want me, or anyone, to take care of her. She was adamant with her expressions and I was a bit scared at first. I questioned if I would be able to serve. Her independence was important to her and she was in no way ready to surrender that by allowing me of all people, to care for her. "Humpf," she made that sound and turned her head away with a snarly attitude. Should I be insulted and decide this wasn't for me? Nah, I'm up for a challenge. Nothing I offered seemed to comfort her on this first day. I wasn't about to give up though.

Being an empath, I could feel her sadness, pain, frustration and desire to have a friend along with something else that went deeper, which I will share later. She was frightened, too.

Over the next few weeks, with diligent patience and compassion, I came to understand her. Over time, she even admitted she liked me. I learned she loved to dance with her French lover who had crossed over many years ago. The romance they shared was better than any movie I have seen. Occasionally, she would speak in French about the love affair, and boy was it juicy! In those moments I was grateful to have studied French so I could understand the passion they shared. She would giggle like a radiant young woman, describing his luscious kisses and how he would caress her. I could almost see her in a beautiful flowing gown and fancy shoes, her hair pulled back in a sophisticated, fashionable bun, so eloquent and graceful as she danced in his arms. Yet in this time her body was frail, weighing a mere ninety pounds, her legs barely supporting her. I could feel how much she longed for those bygone days once again.

Our conversations would go on for hours as I brushed her hair ever so carefully because it was falling out, and massaged her hands gently. The two of us laughed like schoolgirls. She was quite the storyteller and her life was filled with explorations of culture, higher education, lots of romance, family stories and insights of wisdom that even she couldn't quite understand. Sometimes, she would share how disappointed she was with many things and people in life . During these end stages of life, she realized her studies to transcend human nature as an avatar had made her vulnerable. Existing with this terrible disease was mind boggling. She felt it ripped her beliefs apart. "I did not choose this way to die!" she screamed. "How could this be?" Infuriated because she had spent a lifetime searching to gain perspective, truth and divinity and yet knowing there was still more to learn. She was so tired, and on this particular day required a bit more rest. Quietly, I took her throw cover and gently placed it over her lap as her eyes shut closed and she drifted off to sleep.

An avatar incarnates to re-establish the one eternal spiritual truth, and obviously Sylvie had more to experience. We spiral further inward at different life stages. Just when we may think we have awakened, we receive another layer, a deeper lesson to journey through. I would learn over these months how I would be able to serve her beyond anything I would have dreamed. You see, Sylvie knew I could feel what she needed, and I believe that's why our friendship grew exponentially in a very short time.

The weeks would fly by, some days with tropical storms and high winds shaking the palm trees, other times with full rainbows appearing over the house across the street as we sat on her lanai discussing the spiritual development of humanity. Her brilliant mind helped expand my own, yet here she was, still questioning so much. Sylvie was not about to believe just anything and I admired that quality in her. I listened, only offering input or ideas when I felt divinely guided by a higher source - Jesus. This wasn't just any caretaking job; this was care taking the soul. I didn't know it then that this would be the path leading me one day to become a soul purpose sage, helping others find their spiritual truth.

As her body became weaker and deteriorated at a rapid rate over the weeks, we found many moments of gratitude, appreciating the pleasures in life. Especially when I snuck in her favorite chocolates, pâté and Brie. Sylvie wasn't into eating much these days and who was I to limit the delights she longed for that no one else would provide. After all, she had the right to choose what brought her joy.

I can so vividly recall the evening I stayed over

so her kids could celebrate their anniversary. She gently patted my hand as I put her to bed and held the other one firmly. She was gazing into my eyes, feeling oh so tired from this whole situation, and with a soft voice she asked me, "Gloria, did you know I am dying in three months? The doctors told me so. Most of my time is already gone."

I paused, breathing for a moment, wondering how to respond. "What if you lived every day in these months, instead of dying each day?"

"Why," she said, "Since you put it that way – YES! No one told me I could live for three months." The smile on her face lit up her tired blue eyes and together we fell asleep peacefully, holding hands.

An avatar, I would come to learn, equips you with tools to deliberately restructure the beliefs that were patterns of your life. These influence your thoughts, expectations and your actions. They even affect the outcome and the way you perceive them. I guess that is what I was suggesting, so she could explore her existence and reveal a new truth, casting even more light upon her own spiritual consciousness.

Each week her family thought it would be her last, only to call me and say, "Come over, Sylvie wants to spend time with you." Everything was becoming more difficult for her to do, even basic things, and it was hard to watch her physical body failing. Amazingly though, she always found the strength to talk story. Can you believe almost a year had gone by as I watched her wither to barely sixty-five pounds of bones and sagging flesh, yet her spirit was still teaching me about the veil of illusion. No amount of medications could stop her from sharing fun stories and beautiful wisdom.

One day, I could see she was sad, depressed and longing for something. I gently placed her fragile body in the wheelchair and took her outside to her favorite place, the lanai. She wasn't speaking much that day, but she did manage to ask me how I always knew what to do and would I bring my easel outside and paint. She sat quietly observing me with obvious thoughts rolling through her mind. I could see a faraway look taking her somewhere. Her lips began to shape slowly into a smile and she told me another story about the days her father would take her to the museum where he was the art curator. Sylvie had great knowledge about art and saw something in my painting, a talent she recognized from other famous artists. I was not as well-versed, at the time, and frankly thought she was hallucinating from her meds, but accepted the compliment. Then there was complete silence. A deep stillness, an almost unsettling silence. I slowly looked over my right shoulder, frightened she may have stopped breathing only to find her staring at the palm tree blowing in the wind. Her fascination was intriguing, and I knew there was something deeper emerging by the intensity of her eyes. I could sense it. I grabbed my trusty journal and patiently waited. Over these last several months I never went to visit Sylvie without my journal because she was always sharing a multitude of profound insights. I knew, like on that first day I met her, she was about to tell me something. I always intuitively felt her within my own senses and she knew she could count on me.

A whisper floated through the air as I heard, "Will you be with me when I decide to transition?"

I responded, "You just have to call out to me, and I will show up. I promise." Her body was hunched slightly forward in the wheelchair and she just smiled as her face softened with an angelic glow. It was like an aura embraced her entire being. A great look of comfort and peace washed over her.

Her eyes looked up at the wind blowing through the palm trees. She was very quiet, observing, yet

I sensed something was happening energetically. I could literally see the connection between them, no separation. I was ready with my pen to write, knowing she was going to speak.

When I began to write her words, I noticed after a few moments this was a conversation between Sylvie and 'someone', the tree? A higher wisdom? Her French lover waiting for her on the other side of the veil?

"You know you are beautiful, graceful. You use it to seduce."

"You flatter to please and you know it. You have so much to live for."

She would seemingly wait for an answer from the tree, or whoever she was conversing with, smile and continue.

"Things are good and beautiful and always there, graceful palm tree, ever, ever graceful."

"Look at you." ~ Pausing ~

"I can hear you whisper. You can't hide from me. I wouldn't let you."

She spoke very slowly, as if they were engaged in a deep, romantic conversation. Actually, I believe they were. If only I too, could hear the trees speak. The palms would wave to her and each time she would nod her head, just knowing, and continue her conversation.

"You have so much to say, look at you, you just talk." ~ Pause~

"I love you too, I do, I do." ~ Pause ~

"I do, plenty, yes."

I could feel a thread of light connecting them, bonding them and engaging in a divine feminine flow of energy. They were one.

"Look at you, you are trembling. Now calm down."

"You are happy and should be, always." ~ Pause ~

"Gentle, tranquil and beautiful.

"Each of you have a job and yours is to wave your beauty around."

"To give and be blessed. Yes, you are beautiful!"

Just then, Sylvie's blue eyes sparkled in the sunshine as her body took on a vibrant glow and she looked healthy. I had never seen her radiate like this over the last year.

"I am so happy for you and I am happy with you,

Thank you."

"Thank you."

"Ah, look at you, you really are so happy."
~ Pause ~

The skies opened with a gentle mist of rain as she continued. "Ah, the rain, it feels so good and so beautiful,"

"Wet and damp. Yes, I love you always."

"All we ever need to do is ask for it and that reminds me ~ Pause ~ we will get it."

"I know who you are, yes."

"Look at you." (as the tree leaves calm down)

"You have plenty to give and I will always love you."

"Remember that ~ Pause ~ yes."

   As this conversation continued, I was intrigued with the way the leaves seemed to respond to her. I watched her body sit up straighter as she became brighter with what seemed to be an energy from a higher source.

"I like you too, without you, I wouldn't be here."

"This place is good for you I can see that."

"You love nature and it knows it gives you all you need."

She closed her eyes to rest and I felt so blessed to bear witness to this oneness. I felt we were enveloped in a great calm and there was support for both of us. I felt embraced by the magical and loved by the divine. It was so simple to just be, in this loving comfort and to love ourselves from within. Only stillness and love.

Then I wrote, "To embrace our own light and be content with our essential selves, so it is, and I am."

Sylvie responded as if she knew what I was writing, "Because you are love and there to share it ~ there is love everywhere." Her breath became shallow.

"Would this be her final breath?" I thought.

After a long, peaceful pause, she looked over at me and happily smiled. I began to read all of what she said, and she replied, "You write beautifully."

"Ah, but you said all of this, not I," I said.

"Yes, but without you it would not have been put into existence. You see we are all needed."

An avatar has two key theological concepts: God is feminine, and nature is infused with her divine spirit. The whole system of spiritual revelation is based upon a conscious linking and transmission of energy from one aspect of divine manifestation to another, from God in the "secret place of the highest" to the humblest human being struggling on earth. Avatars like Jesus Christ, Buddha, and other sages who walked this earth, have a pre-ordained destiny and a capacity to transmit energy or divine power. We find that during human crisis, these are the ones who bring awakening times forth; following the Law of Compassion, becoming teachers who share messages and insights that will heal, hence illuminating the darkness for others.

The day had been long for both of us and it was time for Sylvie's dinner and for me to go home. Somehow, I knew this was the last time I would see her in this reality. I kissed her gently on her cheek and she grabbed my hand. With no words spoken I heard in my own head, "When it is time, be there for me." I tilted my head as if to say yes, turned away and drove home to prepare for a trip I would be taking to a sacred site on the island the following day.

Oh, how I loved to drive to the west side of the island, taking the long, bumpy, dirt road out to Poli Hale, the sacred site known as the "Portal for

Spirit." That night I laid under the stars while falling into a mesmerizing consciousness shift. My head was spinning and it felt like I leapt into another dimension. I heard Sylvie call out to me. I knew it was the initial feeling I had when I met her. It was to guide her home. She was ready to take that next step and without hesitation I was there to assist her calling. I said, "Take my hand, along with my friend, Jesus." In this moment a divine and powerful energy filled me, a veil was lifted and I felt a revelation, a spiritual peace as she entered a golden path to go home.

Several days later I received a call from her family, telling me that she had passed over with a smile on her face. I imagined she was now dancing with her French lover, who was with her at the portal that night. My friend Carol said to me, "You were at Poli Hale, weren't you?"

"Yes. Sylvie came, and I held her hand," I told her. Carol just 'knew' and was happy that Sylvie wasn't alone the evening she fell into a deep, peaceful sleep.

The doorway had opened for me to continue exploring human consciousness. Spiritual truth was about to take me on a divine assignment. I would have many spiritual revelations over the next few decades. My journey would take me to many sacred sites in the world; not only Hawaii but Egypt, Peru and many other places in this beautiful world. I would study with elders, kahuna and shaman, receive initiations and walk a path of the soul awakening. One day I would be shown how to help others facilitate their soul purpose and help them understand their soul blue print. Had this synchronous meeting been so divinely planned? Absolutely Yes! You see, every event, every person is always teaching us something and if we open our minds to new perspective, we evolve on this healing journey.

As you read the upcoming short stories in this book, I believe you will relate with parts in your own life, a little with each one. Every author began awakening on a path leading them to a spiritual discovery, each one at a different stage in life, yet they all had something in common, like Sylvie.

Each of us have many paths to walk and levels of awakening. If we choose to make choices in each situation that will raise our consciousness, open our hearts and help us find gratitude, forgiveness and compassion, our evolution will continue. No matter what hand we are dealt, we can find the courage within the core of our faith, gain the strength to keep going and find our own path through our healing journey. The effect it will have on our lives and the lives of others undeniably will give us freedom, just like Sylvie saw written on me when we met. Now, it's your turn to explore and meet others who may have an insight or message for you on your *Path of Awakening*.

Awakening to Freedom

Angela Jones Taul, Author
Women Standing Strong Together

I dreamed of the day my
freedom would come,

My thoughts and trauma no
longer to keep me from

The amazing feeling of my
soul becoming alive,

No longer dormant and filled with lies.

Freedom I prayed for, freedom I craved,

Freedom I received once I
let go and believed.

It awakened my Light so I
could spread my wings,

I'm in harmony now and
my soul loves to sing.

Freedom gives me the power to bloom,

Awakening within will give
you the power too.

Dora Sherry is a Champion Badass Survivor in life's challenges.

This multiple time cancer survivor has been shot, stabbed, and lived two years in a wheelchair after being thrown from a third-floor balcony, not knowing if she would ever walk again. There have been many more experiences like this in her life, but without a doubt, the two biggest challenges she has had to survive are the death of her only child at 18 in 1990 and an opiate addiction that has held her prisoner for 40 years.

These would be her toughest battles. She is still battling through it today, all these years later. She would like you all to go through this adventure of exploring who she is, who she was and healing today, that person who still is hurting inside.

Badass Dora got up and out of that wheelchair after two years. She became a third-degree black belt in Kenpo karate. That's how she's gone through everything, especially her son's death; like a champion. Champions don't look back. They concentrate on now and forward. Sometimes they are so strong though, that they forget to take care of that heart and hurt inside of them.

"This is my story. I have had Angels around me through all my life. I thank them for rescuing me from some very deadly situations many times. I thank God for sending those Angels to me. I am thankful that I recognize them in every form. I love God for all the challenges I've had in my life. They have made me the woman I am today. With all my heart, 'If I weren't me, I would wish I was.'

My story is dedicated to all those survivors of life's challenges."

DORA
SHERRY

Author, Inspirational Speaker, Comedian,
Grief Supporter, Supporter of Young
Life Christian Teen Program

© 2020 Original artwork by Candy Lyn Thomen

A Mother's Worst Nightmare

My son, a handsome young man and the love of my life, looked at me and said, "Mom, I know you love God and I'm your only child. What would you do if God asked you to sacrifice me?"

That is not something I ever wanted to hear as I teared up and felt like my chest was going to explode. I had to be honest to my handsome young man and love of my life. God already knew what was in my heart.

I looked at my son and I said, "I don't know son. I do believe my love for God and my faith is strong enough. If He chooses to take you from me for some reason, I will have to find a way to get through the anger. I would think I would still love Him and trust Him; however, I would try to honor your life and thank God for giving you to me." Inside, I wasn't sure about any of it. Although, the words seemed to make sense at the time. Little did, I know one day I would be tested.

It was a day I will always remember as the words repeat in my head for decades. "I love you Mom."

"I love you too sweetheart. Drive safely and be careful. I'll see you when you get home. Remember to wake me up and let me know you're home."

My son was so excited to take his car out for a drive and meet up with some friends for a graduation party. We spent the day shopping even though I was healing from a back injury. He desperately wanted me to go and said, "One day, you will wish I was here, so come shop with me." He was a very happy teenager who felt like a big man now that he had his wheels. Confident, cocky, a big guy excited to party that night. I remember him saying, "If I died tonight, this is the happiest day of my life, hanging out with you." Looking back, I am so glad I managed to pull myself out of bed despite the pills I had taken earlier. I am grateful to have had a wonderful day, the last day I would ever spend with my baby.

He called and woke me up at 2:15 a.m. to say he was sorry he was late and to ask if the boy that was riding in the car with him could stay overnight. He hung up saying, "I love you, Mom."

Then, the dreaded moment came. My test with God would arrive at my house at 7:20 a.m. The cop was a real handsome Italian-looking man in his sharp police officer uniform. At first, I thought my son got into some prank at the party. Instead, he muttered these horrible words I will never forget, "Your son died in a car accident." It was only moments ago I was saying goodbye to my baby, never imagining in a million years it would be the last time. They told me he died at 3:05 a.m., not even an hour after he had called me.

My mind was confused, my heart was pounding, and I screamed, "It couldn't be. This can't be true. You have the wrong house. You have the wrong mother. It can't be my son. It can't be my baby. He can't be dead!" Louder and louder my words blurted, "You're wrong! You are wrong!" I screamed at everyone as my heart was breaking and my mind was snapping. Everything seemed surreal and this could not be possible, no way!

When the detective handed me my son's driver's license, there was no denying it. I fell to my knees and I screamed, "No God, please not my baby. Please, NO!" I worked so hard to bring this little boy into this world. "How could you take him from me, God?" I cried out. "I thought You loved me. I've loved you my whole life, Lord, from the time my daddy told me you were a good God and the ultimate loving father. I've trusted You, but now I'm pissed at You. I loved my Michael so much, how will my heart ever heal from this, why didn't you take me instead?"

It has taken me 30 years to admit I was so pissed off at God. I only just realized it as I was writing this story. I was so ashamed of being mad at God because I was so sure he was a loving God and this didn't feel that way at all. It wasn't very loving to take my only child from me. That's not a loving God. That sounds more like the devil right now. That's right, you heard me! It's kind of being mad at your Dad, even though you love him.

Then, I remembered a few weeks earlier when my son came home from school and asked me what the story of Abraham and Isaac meant. They were going to perform at a play in school. He was supposed to be the voice of God. When Abraham raised the axe to sacrifice Isaac, God was to say, "Wait, I was just kidding." My son asked me what made God change his mind in that split second? I told him that God needed to know Abraham loved God more than anyone or anything on earth and the fact he was willing to sacrifice his son meant he won the test. He got to keep him.

Standing in my living room that day, remembering his question, is probably the only thing that helped me hold it together. That's the day I had to start really loving God and trusting Him; not just believing in Him. My anger at God turned into a deeper faith and a deeper trust. He had prepared me with my own child's question. Yes, it was time for me to seriously question my own faith and devotion to God and to love myself more too.

"Are you okay?" I heard the police officer ask. My mind came back to the reality of what was going on in my living room again. I was sitting on the cold, hard floor rocking back and forth with my knees in a fetal position, dazing off somewhere. Am I okay? What a ridiculous question to ask someone, as I thought about how my whole life was never going to be the same.

My entire life, I had an inner knowledge and feeling I wasn't going to get to keep my son very long. I guess you could say it was a vision or a voice inside of me when I would look at him. It would always say, "Cherish him, because he won't be here long." I would freak out inside when I would think those thoughts. How could I be thinking that about my son? Why would I hear those words? What could I do to prevent this nightmare?

As I sat on the floor, a clear and vivid memory hit me. Two years prior, when he was 16 and had just obtained his license, we were driving past the very spot where he died today. I had the thought in that very moment, "I'm going to lose him soon." Stop saying these things to me in my head! Was I being prepared?

Suddenly, there were tons of people in my house. Friends and family were all loving on me, yet not really knowing what to say. People loved Michael. He was a sweet kid; a big teddy bear and I was always so proud of him. Sure, he gave me the typical headaches, pulling my hair out as a teen when he would get into a bit of trouble. Just like teenagers, he would back talk to me when I took his car keys away as a punishment because he didn't clean his room. He said, "Mom, that's not fair. Ever since I got my car, you've had me by the balls." To which I replied, "That's why they call them the family jewels and I will hold you by them as long as you live in this house." He just growled at me and walked to his room.

This little fighter only weighed 4 ½ pounds when I brought him into this world. His lungs weren't fully developed and even then, I was afraid I might lose this precious angel. My whole life was passing in front of me, like a video. I could hear his laughter and I just wanted to be left alone with my memories of him.

I wanted to slap the next person who gave me words of encouragement. I just wanted to be left alone. Screaming, "Please leave me alone!" I ran as fast as I could to his room, laid on his bed and held one of his stuffed animals.

If you've ever lost someone, you probably know you can smell them. We try to feel close to them one more time. We would do anything to find a way to connect. I locked the door and just cried my heart out. I feared I would be haunted my whole life and never sleep well again. How could I ever sleep again when I couldn't believe this myself! What had I done that somehow made this happen? I truly thought I would be the first person to die of grief. Obviously, God had a greater purpose to keep me here to share this story.

Oh God, I hear the kids, all Michael's friends. They were all in my house all the time hanging out with Michael. I loved having the kids here just hanging out. Now, they're in the other room crying and screaming. I must get up. I must go out there and I must find some way to be strong for them. This is how I became very stoic and very strong. I had to be like a soldier or a general, being the one re-assuring everyone else it was okay. It's quite interesting how we find this strength to console others when we are the ones dealing with a deep loss and so much pain.

The next day, it was time to go to the funeral home. I must pick out clothes for my only son to be buried in. How am I going to do this while I still felt like this was all surreal, questioning how this happened. All I could do was cry nonstop. Thankfully my family helped me get through the process.

The dreaded evening arrived, and my body could not move. I felt like my feet weighed a thousand pounds. If I go, it will be real and I wasn't ready to face this truth. Not ever. Instead, I sat in the car for 45 minutes. It felt like hours and yet, it felt like seconds. All I could think is, "I can't do this!" Over 200 of my son's friends would be there, including my family and friends, holding me up as I walked, bent over, slowly up the aisle to the casket to view my baby for the first time.

When I opened my eyes and looked at the body lying there, it wasn't him. Oh my God. It's not my baby. His face had been damaged so horribly in the accident; it didn't look like him. I was so sure it was all a dream or just a huge mistake. Once I cleared the tears from my eyes, I could see his hair. That's his hair. Oh my God, those are his eyebrows! I knew his lip was cut, because I kept rubbing my lip for 2 days. My lip was raw and almost bleeding. I kept rubbing it, saying something's wrong with his lip. I reached out to touch his lip when I heard people say, "Don't let her touch him. Dear God, don't let her touch his face." Thank goodness the funeral director said, "Let her touch him, that's her baby." I touched his lip and I touched mine and that's the last thing I remember before passing out.

This was much more than I could handle. It was the truth. He really was dead. I woke up in one of those dreary rooms in the funeral home with someone brushing my hair and someone else trying to give me a Xanax. They were telling me my doctor had prescribed it for me today, just in case. It was obvious, common sense that he would fear how I was going to handle it. I remember telling them I cannot tranquilize this away. I must go through it. I must take care of these kids that are here and make sure they're alright. They insisted I take the pill. However, deep inside of me, I was afraid my addiction would resurface. I'm glad I took it though, because it helped. I pulled myself together and walked up to the casket. I stood there as hundreds of people marched past me, each one wanting to give me a hug, trying to console me while hoping they had the right words. I would look at them, seeing the pain in their face, and it would magnify mine because there are no 'right' words.

The children broke my heart, they were so hurt. None of them knew how to handle it, how could they? They were all looking to Mommy Dora to tell them what to do. I hugged each one and I promised them it would be okay. I assured them I was all right and would continue to the next child to do the same. Was God giving me this strength to help others in this moment? How could a grieving mother handle these gut-wrenching moments when she wasn't okay, when she was numb? I just wanted to die.

Then my dad came in. "Oh Daddy," I cried when I heard his voice. "This hurts so bad," I said, while he wrapped his arms around me.

"I know baby, I know," he said. He did know. He

had lost a child too, my 10 year old brother when I was very young. He could understand the depth of this horrid and empty feeling for sure. A man of God, I remember how strong my father was when my brother got hit by a drunk driver while riding his bicycle. It all came back so clearly; even how he held the driver in his arms, forgiving him and consoling him while it was his turn to bury a child.

Today as I write this I realize how many years I had stuffed my grief way down to help console others. Perhaps, because I saw Daddy be so strong, always helping others; I thought this is what was expected of me too. I had no idea how many emotions would surface writing this to help someone else. I crashed again, went into hiding and cried all night long. The healing process is beginning and finally, I know my addiction to pain meds numbed me out. I am trusting God to help me through this process. I am trusting this healing journey.

The funeral is a blur, as I cannot remember most of it and barely know how I got to the grave site. I do recall some of the words my brother-in-law said at the eulogy, but I don't remember most of it because I was still in shock. Everyone mentioned he did a wonderful job. Huh? A wonderful job and my baby is gone? That doesn't even equate in my head.

What's so wonderful about all of this?

I barely remember sitting at the graveside, staring at the casket and not hearing anything they were saying. I had so many thoughts flying inside of my head. So much pain screaming inside of me. Tears flowing, my mascara dripping down my face. This can't be happening. I remember someone trying to hand me a rose or flower from the casket as we started to leave the cemetery. I abruptly slapped it away. "I'm sorry," I said. "I guess I'm a little angry." I didn't care in that moment what anyone thought. Yes, I was angry.

Finally, it was a relief to have everyone gone. Actually, I felt a little better not having to hold myself up for them. My son's friends were the ones who made me laugh, telling funny stories about Michael. We chuckled, enjoyed our memories and then it was time for them to leave. Once the door opened, I saw the most beautiful sight, something that would make me feel closer to my son than I could have ever felt in life. It was his first sign of letting me know he is my angel and still here.

One perfect flower. I had waited six years for just one flower on this little peony bush. My son had even taken a picture of it a few days before his accident, in case something happened to it and it didn't bloom. It had about 50 bulbs on it and only one in the middle started to grow. It was showing a little light pink petal starting to peek out. We were all so excited we were finally going to get one flower.

The day it was planted I remember saying, "Dear God, I just need one flower." I knew I would have a world-famous flower one day if I just had faith. Just give me one flower, dear God, to show the world. There it was, blooming for Michael. Michael's friend said, "No that's blooming for you. That's Michael saying, 'There's your one flower Mom.'" My prayers were answered. God is there for us in the right timing.

That evening, when everyone was gone, I sat and read pages of all the beautiful notes his friends gifted me. It was such a precious feeling to know how much they loved him and how he taught them to be family. In that moment, I was a proud mama.

At 1:30 in the morning, I remembered the flower and felt compelled to go outside. I sat in the driveway holding this precious flower to my face as I cried into it. I can still smell it thirty years later and can still feel the dew drops on my cheeks, my chin, and lips. I whispered into the flower, "I love you too baby and I'm going to miss you." It was amazing how close I felt to him in this moment. Thank you for being my

Angel on earth and thank you for being my Angel in heaven.

Sometimes bad things happen to good people. We must trust God knows why and that's all we need to know. I know today, I'm glad I had that little boy for eighteen years; some never have that blessing. I choose to thank God for that and not be mad anymore. I choose now to deal with my grief and start healing. I choose to put a forty year opiate addiction away and not be sick and tired anymore. I was sleeping my life away; doctors told me I had "Sleeping Beauty" syndrome. Yes, opiates took over my life in so many ways. I pray now for the strength to keep living with this freedom and burying this addiction forever.

Writing this story and going back to that scary place, the place I was so afraid to go to for thirty years, has given me so much healing. It has taken so much of that hole away from my heart. I don't need pills anymore. I just need to start living my life now and start trusting my Angels when they talk to me. I have to stop ignoring them like I've been doing all these years. They've been screaming at me from everywhere while I just keep covering my head and ignoring them, lying to myself and others. Now, I'm going to rise and fly with the angels. I'm going to make the best of my life from here on out.

The only consolation I have now is knowing he's here with me. He is my Guardian Angel and he shows himself all the time. I'm always writing stories about how the number 44 appears in my life. That was his favorite number. When he was a little baby and reaching for building blocks, barely able to sit up, he would reach for two fours. When I asked him one time why he loved that number so much, he said, "I don't know mom. I just always have. There's just something about that number that feels special to me."

I feel Michael was the one who threw my pain pills in the washing machine a few months ago. I was thinking about writing a book, but honestly, how could I if I wasn't being honest with myself? That morning, I had my pills laid out on the bed, counting them, when the doorbell rang. I quickly covered them up with the sheet. I didn't want anyone to see my pile of pills, and I also didn't want my cat eating them. You know that saying "It all comes out in the wash?"

Later in the day, I threw my sheets in the washing machine, completely forgetting the pills were rolled up in them. Typical of me forgetting because I had spent decades high, sleeping or numbed out. I felt sick to my stomach when I went to look for my pills. For an opiate addict, this is a panic situation, when you can't find your drugs. I had just refilled the prescription, so they had to be somewhere. I prayed and caught a glimpse of something on the floor. "Thank you God," I was saying as I quickly got down on my hands and knees to pick up those precious little pearls. Evidently the pills had fallen on the ground when I threw the sheets in the washing machine earlier that day.

Frantically I sorted through them, following them like a trail of bread crumbs. "There have to be more, maybe near my bed," I thought. Yes, there were some more. I found myself desperately holding onto those pills, my hands trembling, like they were my lifeline. I continued searching all around my bedroom floor with a flashlight, like a kid looking for hidden presents during Christmas.

The next day, I woke up and realized I needed to stop taking these evil pills. I was getting so sick and tired of being sick and tired. I knew eliminating and weening myself off them would not be easy. I would experience a detox, like the one I had gone through years prior. This was serious, but I was more ready than ever to stop this madness. I was missing out on life, my friends, relationships and probably much more God had planned for me. My addiction is a cycle, like the wash and it was going out now.

I have a better vision of my future, supportive friends and help, including my angel baby who all remind me that God is here for me every day.

Thirty years later, after my son's death, I am realizing I didn't get to grieve or forgive myself. I'm still grieving my son, and for the first time I'm feeling it. I love to tell funny stories about Michael because he was such a comedian and such a cute kid. This was my way of stuffing the grief so far inside and the way I had been drowning my pain with pills. It was only now it became clear how far down the rabbit hole I went all these years. Michael had been sending me a wake-up call for years, sending signs with his favorite number 44, I just had to pay attention. He was showing me God didn't give up on me. All these years, he was trying so diligently with signs to have faith and hope. Michael was saving me when I couldn't save myself and he was not giving up. Thank God he brought all the right people and circumstances in my life to wake up.

Don't be afraid to grieve like I did. The fear will destroy you. It's relieving beyond imagination and I wish I had known this earlier in my life.

"Keep crying," I would say to myself, "tears are healing." God gives them to us, not just to anoint our eyes but to clear our hearts. My father once said, "If you didn't have grief, you wouldn't have love. Concentrate on the memories." Dad was a minister who said, "If tears were only there to lubricate your eyeballs and keep them moving, they wouldn't need to fall down your face. Tears fall because that's the wash cycle." It really does all come out in the wash.

It was now making sense how I was going to help so many parents in life get through the loss of their precious babies. God was going to align me with a church where I would receive support and strength, and the knowledge that I would survive. I realize my son Michael has been watching over me all these years and now I made the decision, finally, to deal with my opioid addiction. I know this will be a healing journey and I am confident with the support I have. My path will awaken me to a higher purpose.

I am so grateful for every angelic sign my son sent to me for decades and I thank God I'm alive to share this story with you. Look for the angelic signs in your life, they are always there. Remember to pay attention. The ones you love are there to help you now.

Message of Awakening

Tina Mast
Author, Angel Communicator
Women Standing Strong Together

For most of us, the path to awakening has been long and at times, challenging. When your purpose and passion are being timely revealed to you, you begin to understand why your life has taken this necessary path.

This excitement and enthusiasm you feel propels you in a way you never knew. Hold fast and enjoy those delicious, new discoveries. Savor that exciting understanding of who you are and why you're here.

As you learn to know parts of you that were once a mystery, you'll feel a deeper connection to your heart, your life and

your soul. Growing in this new phase will give you an intense feeling of finally meeting yourself for the first time.

Grant yourself permission to look back on those times that seemed so overwhelming, as you start to finally understand why things happened to you the way they did. Accept why certain people have been part of your life and why dreams didn't happen right away or even at all.

This is a great time of growth and learning. Know that part of your purpose it to help others on their journey. I cherish the times I've been able to help others by stepping into my authenticity and being the person that I myself needed when I was struggling to find my way. As you share and encourage others on this awakening journey, you'll be shown new parts of yourself and the role you play on this beautiful earth. You're beginning to meet the person you knew you were all along.

This is one of the first steps on your beautiful path of awakening and exciting times are part of future. Understand that part of learning to know your soul, you will be stretched outside of your comfort zone and I can tell you from experience, it'll be incredibly scary and amazingly magnificent all at the same time.

Love and light to you all!

"*Blessed are those who give without remembering and blessed are those who take without forgetting.*"

Bernard Meltzer

Jean was a late bloomer to the Healing Arts. Growing up there was no talk of meditation, yoga or self- care, besides the usual brushing of teeth and cleaning behind the ears. She got a BA in Fine Arts and has always had a passion for creative endeavors which landed her the opportunity to illustrate a series of seven children's books. Getting married and having three sons kept her plenty busy, while her husband started a screen-printing business that she has now worked at for 27 years.

In order to release some energy and learn something new, Jean took up Martial Arts and practiced it for 8 years until reaching Black Belt at the age of 42. She found a calling to explore several healing arts modalities such as Body Talk, Reiki, EFT Tapping and graduated from the Institute for Integrative Nutrition when she was 53. That same year she went back to college to become a Licensed Massage Therapist (the only gray -haired grandmother in the class!) where she discovered the beauty and effective power of healing hands.

It's been the ten years of studying and becoming an Emotional Freedom Techniques Practitioner. It has captured Jean's heart and has given her great joy, helping people release limiting beliefs so they can reach their goals and live life to the fullest. This tapping technique gives people the choice to take charge of their own healing, releasing fears, pain, grief, anger, and sadness. An extraordinary tool available at their own fingertips.

It's never too late!

Email contact: jeandansak@live.com

JEAN
DANSAK

Healing Arts Professional
Author, Artist, Photographer

Message of Hope from
JEAN DANSAK

"Where flowers bloom, so does hope."
Lady Bird Johnson

Beauty can spring forth amongst devastation.

Flowers still bloom on a battlefield.

As chaos disrupts our tidy sense of stability,
we can be guided and uplifted by love.

When blinded by fear, look in the
darkness for the shining light where
compassion and kindness abound.

Transcend beyond the material to a place of
simplicity and oneness to bloom in spite of it all.

2

As Good as Ever

Dear Mom,

Guess what I found in the back of the closet today? That box you gave me ten years ago when you first started forgetting the right words. You gave all six of us a box filled with all the things you saved from our childhoods. You had sorted everything and packed it up so we wouldn't have to do it someday. Sadly, I think you knew a time was coming when you wouldn't be able to do it.

I opened my box and spent the next two hours poring over a collection of certificates, report cards, newspaper clippings, paperwork, and lovingly hand-made cards. She even kept the letters I had written home from college. It cost less to buy a stamp than make a long distance phone call back then. My, how things have changed… so much more than I could have ever imagined!

There was my life, neatly packed in a box; all the memories you kept so as not to forget. But that's exactly what you did, Mom. Forget me.

One year into your forgetfulness, I was standing in your kitchen where you had served thousands of meals. I opened the manila envelope that held the results from your psychological evaluation. "Significant cognitive decline" wrote the doctor who tested you. You had taken the same test the year before because you were having trouble with word recall. We had all noticed it. At first, you would laugh it off and we would play a guessing game; trying to fill in what was missing and not knowing which sentence would turn into a game of charades. The test had been repeated to compare results, which devastatingly showed enough decline to warrant a diagnosis…. Alzheimer's.

So, Mom, by giving me that box of memories, you were being so much more than considerate. You were being realistic. You knew what the road ahead would bring while I enveloped myself in a cocoon of denial; denying this was really happening, because surely you had done nothing in your life to merit such a cruel fate! A childish ideal that all things should be fair. I was mad, but more than anything, I was in shock. The kind of shock that bars all emotion and protected me from thinking beyond each day. A self-indulgent yet ignorant belief that time might stand still and nothing else would change. You had still been doing fine on your own; shopping for groceries, making your meals and still meticulously taking care of the house. You were holding onto every shred of what you could still do right. No one could tell from the outside looking in, what you had already lost behind your beautiful blue eyes and compassionate sweet smile.

One of the exercises in your testing was to draw the face of a clock. It sounds simple to do, but surprisingly your drawing looked like a Salvador Dali masterpiece; a melted, twisting clock face. Dali's surrealistic painting of similar looking clock faces is fittingly titled "The Disintegration of the Persistence of Memory." This was what the next three years would bring. We all stepped into the surreal reality of your disintegration, your confusion, your forgetting…. and your loss.

Before I lost you though, Mom, you lost me.

I can clearly remember the day it happened. We were sitting in the dining room with jigsaw puzzle pieces strewn across the table. You were able to sort the pieces by color and I was putting the border together first. You picked up a piece and examined it from all angles, held it, hovering it over all the others, not quite knowing what to do with it and said to me, "Does your mother like to do puzzles?" I took a moment before responding. "Yes, yes she does," I said with a convincing smile. In that stolen moment, which seemed like a lifetime (my lifetime), I screamed in my head, "Mom, it's me! I'm right here. YOU are my mother! Don't you remember?"

I had learned though, it was useless to try and correct and doing so only made you feel embarrassed and confused. No abracadabra trick was going to open the impenetrable vault which held the missing pieces. That was when I came to accept the fact that you no longer knew me as your daughter. You never again called me by my name.

This made me wonder, Mom, if you could forget me, then who am I?

The most important person in my life; the one who bore me, who named me, who cradled me, who raised, taught, supported and loved me, thought I was a stranger.

I'm writing this letter to you now, Mom, as a form of healing, as you have been dead for six years. God, I can't stand that word. Dead. The word sits in my throat like a stone; too low to spit out, too high to swallow; so final, with no room for interpretation. At least the term 'passed' sounds like you have passed to a different place, dimension or time, but still exist. The term gone sounds like you have gone somewhere else, a vacation maybe, but able to check back in now and then, heaven knows you deserved one.

Even still, Mom, I expect to run into you at the grocery store like we did sometimes. It was an unexpected bumping into that let me know you were never far away. After you passed, it took a while to stop thinking of you as being sick and to start remembering you again as vibrant and healthy.

I remember when I was young, the butterfly kisses goodnight, you belting-out show tunes when we did the dishes, and you sending us out to run around the house ten times when we got in your hair. I remember you being the only person I have ever known who never gossiped and whose home was a haven for whoever needed to sit around the kitchen table at any hour and find a compassionate ear.

So, I still wait for an unexpected bumping into, and if that's only possible in a dream or through a message, I'll gladly take it.

In the process of your decline and passing, I had an awakening that allowed me to accept what was happening to your physical body. The undeniable belief that your spirit has been with me the whole time has been crucial, because the spirit is eternal. It is your spirit I feel, and it gives me peace while I'm still in this material world to deal with everything else that distracts me from pure love such as anger, hate, jealousy, fear, guilt, and sadness. It also allows me to open my heart to joy, love, courage, forgiveness and hope. I know I will have distracting emotions which will cause disruption in my energy system, but I have many tools in the healing arts to keep my energy flowing freely.

Mom, if someone were to ask me how I could accept you forgetting me, I would have to say it's the result of Emotional Freedom Techniques, that tapping thing we've done together. EFT founder Gary Craig says, "The cause of all negative emotion is a disruption in the body's energy system." That disruption could be caused by an event in your life where you created a belief about yourself. Initially, that belief could serve you by protecting you from being hurt again, but eventually it doesn't serve a purpose anymore and will be a disservice by holding you back. For instance, when I was doing a speech on stage in seventh grade, some kids laughed at me. For a long time after that event I believed that talking on stage in front of people wasn't safe and I was terrified of it. EFT tapping reduced that fear and I no longer felt like I had to live by the beliefs of a self- conscious teenager.

Let me give you an example of EFT. Simply start by acknowledging an event and/or emotion that is causing a problem. Test how intensely it feels on a scale from 1-10. Say a phrase of self-acceptance despite the issue. Tap on 9 different points on the head, face, and body with fingertips. Test again to see if the intensity has reduced. Repeat as necessary until the initial emotional intensity is very low or gone.

While it sounds ridiculously simple, I have ten years of practice in it and have witnessed amazing, unbelievable results.

EFT helped both of us along the way to be more peaceful in dealing with your illness. I was grateful to have this tool for you and feel it allowed you to deal more calmly with the situation.

Eventually you lost interest in eating. We tried the best we could to cajole you into your favorites or something new. Sometimes, when you weren't sure what to do with a certain food, it would end up as some type of sculpture or neatly placed around the outside of your plate. Again, it's hard feeling responsible for something you don't have any control over. I felt like I was failing you, Mom, as you kept dropping weight. I had to figure out something to do for myself. I remembered something I learned in a training. It is a wonderful Hawaiian forgiveness prayer called Ho'oponopono that really helped me reconcile with the feeling of failing you. There are four steps to this prayer which involves repentance, forgiveness, gratitude, and love. This helped me heal from feeling any responsibility for your decline, I could say:

"I'm sorry for any responsibility I had in failing you."

"Please forgive me."

"Thank You."

"I love you."

It's a lovely and powerful tool.

I am so fortunate you were such a great Mom. You raised six kids, all with a deep sense of responsibility and ultimately, the reason we were able to work so well together to keep you in your home. My three sons were grown when you were diagnosed, and I found myself right back in the role of being a caretaker with you. The weight of that responsibility felt like a ton of bricks sometimes, with all the doctor appointments, medications, getting you to eat, finding things to stimulate your mind, dealing with the emotional reactions to your illness, and the fear of not doing everything possible. Even when I wasn't "on duty", the responsibility remained as a feeling of being closed in, like I was in a room that was getting smaller and smaller. When this happened, I knew some breathing exercises would help, along with some guided meditation and yoga. All these coping mechanisms reduced the stress and gave me a renewed sense that we could get through this. It is my hope that this experience will help others that are also caretakers of their loved ones find a way to cope easier.

Caring for people was who you were. You'd had the same responsibility caring for our grandmothers, yet you never acted like it was a burden, but a way of life.

What a cruel joke, that after a lifetime of giving and giving and wanting to give more, this was your fate. That was a hard pill to choke on and attempt to swallow. It just sat there in my throat. Not surprisingly, the same sensation I get when I refer to you as being dead.

Fortunately, I could use the tapping to release that block and help get me past the anger, and resentment, and hate toward this unfair illness. My choice, and priority, was to make you feel safe and loved.

You raised amazing children and two of my siblings were able to live in your house with you as they took over your full-time care when you could no longer be alone. It was a special thing for our family to have this connection and support from each other in taking care of you. There is no doubt you would be proud of all of us. During this time, I was in massage school and I was glad to have hands on tools which helped us both to feel more relaxed. You loved your neck and shoulders massaged and of course your feet!

I can't imagine people having to do the job while dealing with a loved one who is very angry and bitter. You blessed us by maintaining your very sweet disposition throughout your whole illness.

This is why it's so important caregivers have access to as many tools as they can; to get through the hard times with as much grace and ease as possible. This experience helped me to learn so much and now I can help others too.

In times of overload I found a wonderful healing exercise called "Morning Pages" developed by Julie Cameron, author of *The Artist's Way*. It is an exercise to do first thing in the morning, before doing anything else, while all the thoughts of the dream state are still floating around in your mind. Have paper and pen available near your bed and fill three complete pages with handwritten notes about everything and anything that pours out of your head; a purging of sorts. Don't think, don't correct, don't judge, don't stop. If it's in your head, let it out! This exercise really helped me to start the day lighter and relieved; to have no stone left unturned. It also helped me see underlying things that I didn't realize were bothering me and gave me a chance to address them. These thoughts and emotions were nothing I would want anyone else to read so I would throw them in the fireplace.

Mom, I learned from you at a young age how to be a caretaker by the way you took care of us all. We didn't have a lot, but you and Dad made sure we had everything we needed. You had no vacations, no retreats, and no spas. You never had a break between the kids, the grandparents, and then taking care of Dad before he died. You barely had any time between being a caretaker to needing care yourself.

I never told you about this, but one day when you were well and in the midst of caring for both grandmothers at your house, I was at a stop light in town and saw you going the other way toward home. You had the most peaceful, gentle smile on your face. I wondered, "How can she look so serene? She could be angry, resentful, overwhelmed." Instead, you were in your element, a veritable angel on earth. It's that exact look on your face that I remember every time I think of you. It overrules any memories of less than ideal moments because none of us is that perfect. Of course, when we were kids you had your over-tired, at your wits end, 'fed up to here' moments; all natural responses. On the rare occasion that something upsetting happened, you might blurt out a "Darn it!" If you were really mad it would be a "Darn it ALL!" It would shock me as a kid but now, the memory makes me smile with glee, knowing that you were human, after all.

What were your tools, Mom? It wasn't in your vocabulary to discuss self-care, being as selfless as you were. I regret that we never talked about it. As great a role model as you were to me, Mom, I'm afraid I wasn't well equipped to handle being a young mother to three boys in four years. I felt the patience gene had passed me by like a semi on the highway in the middle of the night and the stress train had pulled into the station.

If only "Darn it ALL" was the worst thing I ever said. If only I could have controlled my tone and volume of my voice. If only I could go back in time and do it over with the tools that I have now. But we can't be ruled by 'if only'. I can, however, do some tapping on the 'if only' thoughts and how they still affect me now. I can't necessarily control what happens on the outside but have learned that I am the master of how I choose to react.

I want to let you know, Mom, how important my energy healing tools have been in dealing with and healing through the process of your illness, death, and beyond. I'm positive that it helped us both and continues to help me with losing you in the physical and knowing you in the spiritual.

There's just so much to learn from the healing arts that can improve the quality of life. The more I studied the more I knew I would be a lifelong learner. I've discovered that all the modalities pretty much share the same goal from many different fascinating directions, which is homeostasis. Homeostasis is the ability of the body to obtain and maintain a state of balance. When in balance, the body has the great ability to heal itself. We can find balance by acknowledging what we feel in our mind and body. The tools which could have changed my life as a young mother were fortunately the tools I needed and used during the most painful years of my life - the slow and devastating loss of you, Mom.

Even though we were able to keep you in your home for years after your diagnosis, you had a fall and broke your hip. You needed care other than just love and I'm sorry we couldn't take you home again. In a short ten days after being safe at home you were quickly facing the final stretch in a facility. We weren't ready to let you go yet.

The hospice center was quiet and beautiful, surrounded by woods. The staff made us feel so welcome and comfortable as we streamed in and out. You were surrounded by your whole family for days. Coming and going, telling stories, crying, laughing, singing your favorite songs. On the day they told us it would be your last - a dismal, dreary March day - you hadn't opened your eyes in a few days, except maybe briefly. I remember looking at you there, so frail and vulnerable, kept on morphine to fight the pain. I thought of the fear in your eyes the last time you had opened them and thought to myself, "You can do this, Mom."

Throughout the day we had all noticed out the window a small splash of color that stood out against the leafless gray trees. Red. It was a lone male cardinal. The only signs of life to be seen out there. It hung out all day at the edge of the woods over 100 feet away. Several of us commented on seeing it from the large windows in the family lounge where there was a cozy fireplace. We had hung the big picture of Dad in your room where you could see it if your eyes were open. His favorite bird was the cardinal, which was also the name of the town baseball team. Remember how he loved the Cardinals team?

In your last hour, Mom, you managed to turn the most painful time in our lives into the most beautiful as you opened those blue eyes and looked directly into the eyes of each of your children, one by one, as we took turns sitting with you, holding your hands. You left this material world with the whispered word love on your lips, over and over in a faint voice. Love, love, love. You wanted to make sure we knew that you indeed did know us.

While taking your last breaths, which had

become further and further apart, there was a little scratching sound at the window. We barely heard it through swallowed sobs and sniffles. There, the red cardinal clung to the windowsill, patiently looking in. Dad was waiting to greet you.

I want to thank you, Mom, for all that you taught me about how to live and how to die. As always, with grace and ease, and that it's okay to be afraid of something and do it anyways.

I wrote the following after Mom passed and before the memorial service.

"As Good as Ever."

A few weeks after arranging the service, I had a vivid dream. In this dream, I was talking with my mother in her kitchen (of course). I believe she was giving me some good advice. Her voice was clear and her words unfaltering. She looked healthy and strong. It seemed perfectly normal.

In this dream, I began to wonder why we were planning a memorial service for Mom when she was right here? I was in a quandary about what to do, so I called the minister to say, "We need to cancel the service. We are sorry to have taken your time, but our mother is as good as ever!" All seemed right with the world.

As I slowly awoke, I maintained that peaceful feeling. My world was back to normal. There was no cavernous hole in my heart. I could go on as usual. Phew! I took a deep breath. As the cobwebs of sleep slowly cleared, it dawned on me that it was, in fact, only a dream. My mother was not in her kitchen, she was not going to answer her phone if I needed her, and I could not talk to her again. The empty feeling returned. What kind of cruel joke was this dream?

As I began my day, everything proceeded as usual except for the memory of that dream. I was missing something and then finally, I got it.

Thank you, Mom, for letting me know! You let me know that you will always be there for me, you will continue to give me good advice when I call for it and that my heart will be filled with wonderful memories of growing up safe and loved, with humor and compassion. I am so thankful for your message and will always be open to hearing from you.

Thank you most of all for letting me know that now and forever more, you are as good as ever!

I love you,

Your daughter

Awakening

Is not changing

Who you are,

But discarding

Who you are not.

Deepak Chopra

Jen was born and raised in New Jersey and spends all of her "free" time at the Jersey Shore. An intuitive medium, empath, certified Angel Card reader and Reiki Master, Jen loves to teach and share her gifts with her treasured clients and friends. Jen continues to challenge herself by seeking new experiences and projects and her dream would be to someday own a little "rock shop" by the ocean.

A dog rescue advocate, Jen volunteers a lot of her time to various dog rescues. Her connections with animals, especially dogs, since childhood has brought her years of joy and contentment.

In her free time, Jen enjoys time with family and friends, sketching and learning to play the guitar. You can be sure to find her in her favorite beach chair in the summertime with a good book in hand.

Workshops and classes are always being scheduled. Jen's next adventure will be a series of children's books.

Email – cairojen@gmail.com

JEN
CAIRO

Intuitive Medium, Empath,
Certified Angel Card Reader,
Reiki Master

"I dedicate this story to my soul tribe...with me through it all, the laughter, the tears and all in between. I'm forever grateful to you all...."

Drawing by Jen Cairo

An Empath's Awakening

What makes someone look deeper into their spirituality? Is it the search for the ultimate enlightenment? There is so much sadness and pain in the world that it's nice to think there is something bigger than ourselves. I would imagine many of us might feel this way and even discover at some point in our lives a deeper purpose.

Growing up, my world was confusing. I was the kid who sat watching the leaves go down the sewer drain during rainstorms, who was fascinated by ant hills, ladybugs, and spider webs. My feelings did not make sense to me.

As a child, I was never comfortable in my own

skin, always feeling quite different from everyone around me. While other kids were riding their bikes and playing, I was noticing the beauty and wonder in nature. There was this feeling of just knowing things, feeling everything deeper, wanting to be at peace without all the noise from the outside world. I didn't know if other kids had this way of relating to the world. Perhaps you can?

There would come a day, however, when I would more fully understand what being a highly sensitive person meant and why I never felt part of this world, in the same way I thought others did. I guess I took it for granted everyone was the same, only to realize we each have a unique gift.

Imagine being a child knowing what others were feeling, anger, happiness, sickness. All those big emotions were a lot for me to absorb. As a child there was no way for me to understand what I was experiencing. It became easier to keep to myself. Protected in my own private space made me feel safer, more able to cope with what I was feeling.

Let me take you on a journey into my secret world of make believe, into my playroom, the place I kept all my games and toys. There was this big, heavy, wooden closet door and when I would open it, my own creative world would come to life. My imagination was magical, and I created new adventures all the time. Even back then, I loved writing my own story, choosing how my playtime was going to go. Having absolute control over my make-believe world made me feel happy and content.

I remember laying on the floor, looking at my little plastic animals in the closet. I would take myself to a faraway place, like on African safari. I was the ring master and they all came to be with me. In the real world, kids were mean and didn't get along. So, it was magical to have everyone in my world playing nicely. Now, I realize my world of make-believe was really me creating the things I wanted in my real life.

As adults, daydreaming replaces our make-believe worlds. I ask, is it deeper than that? The answer is, simply, yes. We still have the same creative mind that we did as children. Only now, as adults, we are tuning in more to the outside world and maybe feeling a deeper connection to all living things. It's natural for our minds to want to go to a place we feel comfort and happiness, drowning out the mundane "noise" of daily life.

As a child, I felt happy walking the nature trails

in the woods by my house. Nature helped calm me down and relieved my anxiety. It felt magical walking through the rustling leaves, kicking them around and listening to the birds chirping. For hours, I would disappear into my own hidden paradise. Nature became my healer, my spiritual place, my safe haven to escape life's stresses. It's the same way now that I am older. In fact, the need to be outdoors, in nature, has only gotten stronger. Do you ever notice how you feel more balanced and peaceful when you are in nature? Some prefer the ocean, others the mountains, or perhaps gardening at home.

Throughout childhood, my ultimate comfort zone was at the ocean on the New Jersey shore. Driving with my family, I would get excited as soon as we crossed over the big bridge. Smelling the tang of salt in the air and hearing the waves was pure heaven. There was always something so soothing about being near the water, something which made me feel at peace in my soul.

The ocean grounded me and spending time by the water made me feel alive. Being a shy, quiet child, I would come out of my shell, feeling free and invincible! I would sit by the water's edge, making drip-castles as the sounds of the sea seemed to make everything right. When I wasn't building castles in the sand, I'd swim out into the water and ride the waves back in, over and over, until the lifeguards left for the day. This free-flowing, creative play occupied me for hours on end. Running down the beach with my kite sailing in the air behind me, I imagined what it would be like to be riding on top of it.

Some of my best childhood memories were made on those beaches. To this day as an adult, the need to be near the water is unwavering. The ocean became my church, the place where I connected to my inner self, quiet my mind and prayed.

As I grew older, I was feeling lost in my own world. I became quite rebellious and often unapproachable. My shield was so thick, I believe people read me wrong sometimes. At times, I even challenged my own guardian angels, ignoring my gut feelings and purposely doing things I knew I shouldn't; certainly, testing fate and my faith.

Between my religion and the people around me, I didn't know what to believe growing up. As a result, my already lagging self-confidence worsened. In school it became a huge issue, creating many of my problems. I began to hand out with the "tough" crowd because it made me feel safer.

Then my mom died from breast cancer. How could God let this happen to me? As shocking as this loss was for me, I was not as emotional as people may have expected. Oh yes, I was angry at God! Somehow on some deeper level, I knew He would get me through it. Things were so jumbled and there were so many emotions, I wasn't ready or able to process. To make matters worse, not only was I feeling my own emotions I was feeling those of everyone else. It just didn't seem fair. The entire situation, along with the onslaught of unfamiliar emotions, was overwhelming and scary. Yet through it all, I felt God holding me up. A day would come where I would be guided to learn what it meant, how to shield myself and help others.

Even though I was feeling a raging turmoil inside, I rarely showed my emotions outward. As part of my upbringing, I had always felt the need to "be strong". After the death of my mom, I felt like I was dying inside. There was no way I would ever have admitted it to anyone, not even to myself. Never one who shared or talked a lot, I pushed away anyone who tried to get close, becoming short-tempered and withdrawn. I felt like no one could understand what I was going through.

Would I ever make sense of all of this and find my

place? Was there a greater purpose to come out of all of this? If so, please tell me. I grew up Catholic in a time of expectations and pressure to be the perfect Catholic. I felt there shouldn't be so much pressure to be close to God. My family went to church every week. I never really connected with my faith. I was taught to follow certain rules, and if I broke them, I may not get into heaven. I believed in God, there was no doubt. To say I was confused by the words spoken as I sat in church on Sundays was an understatement.

No matter how hard I tried in school I just couldn't focus. Looking back now, I believe I had A.D.D. (attention deficit disorder) as a child. My teachers said it was because I wasn't interested. That wasn't true at all, I was interested! It was always so embarrassing to be called on in class and not have the answers.

I struggled academically, and my social awkwardness eventually attracted the bullies. It started in elementary school; being made fun of because I was quiet and didn't really fit in with any of the "cliques". Having tons of friends was never important to me. I had a handful of close friends, which was all I needed. I was always those special few that helped me get through.

I found one saving grace in it all. Music. Music came easy to me. The clarinet, with its smooth, gentle tones, somehow helped me relax my mind and focus better. Music was my medication. It grounded me, like the ocean had when I was a child. Even though I knew I was smart, academically I always had to work harder. Music gave me a sense of peace. When I played the clarinet, I was the one making the instrument sound beautiful. My family enjoyed hearing me play and for the first time I felt successful. Later in life I learned for people with A.D.D., music can bolster their attention and improve focus. Now it makes perfect sense why music is such a powerful outlet for me.

Fast forward to the present…. Watching my own children grow. I started reminiscing about my own childhood. I began to wonder if it was my faith which guided me through those former days. I became more inquisitive as my memories sprang to life, raising questions I now wanted to find answers to.

The universe had been teaching me more than I could have imagined, and all my experiences were designed to nurture my own soul purpose. Things were falling into place, although I wasn't able to see it just yet.

As it often happened, more synchronicities began to appear. , guiding my path. With each new awareness that filtered in, I became more curious about my feelings and what I had experienced growing up. I started reading articles describing some of the ways empaths felt, and I began to realize this could be me. The articles spoke of how empaths become overwhelmed by the emotions and feelings of the people around them, unable to determine what is their own and what belongs to others. I learned having all those feelings and emotions without boundaries, and no knowledge of how to cope, made things difficult for me. No wonder I often felt anxious, not knowing what to do with everyone's feelings. No wonder I hid in my own world.

Not too long after, I began the journey of learning more about empaths. I discovered I was a highly-sensitive being. I began to acknowledge the fact I was an empath. That's when things really started to connect. Empaths are highly sensitive to the emotions of others, often feeling the same emotions as those they are surrounded by or near. They often see the world differently than others, are misunderstood by many and perhaps called crazy or weird. After taking the first step by acknowledging I was an empath, I started to better understand how to be in charge of my own energy and create healthier boundaries. This meant letting go of toxic energies, learn how to use my gifts. I was to bring them into the world the way the Universe intended and help others.

Little did I know I was being led to people who could help me navigate through all my feelings, perceptions, and emotions. Like my neighbor who lived down the road for 20 years. We didn't really know each other; we only knew our kids played together. A few years ago, she invited me to a meditation session, and we started to communicate more. How crazy is that? Did the universe have a greater plan for me, one I couldn't see during my adolescence? How many signs did I or we miss each day of our lives?

My first invitation was to a spiritual development circle, where like-minded people get together to share ideas and experiences. They also explored their gifts in a safe environment. This came at the perfect time in my crazy life. I was feeling especially stressed, hectic, frazzled, and overwhelmed. A friend told me she thought I could benefit from the circle. She mentioned we would be doing a guided meditation. I never thought I'd be the "meditating" type since my mind was always buzzing, going a million miles per hour. I liked to call it "monkey mind". How was I going to calm my thoughts long enough to get any benefits, I wondered? Hesitant, I went to the circle that night with an open mind. What I received in return was a great experience. Guided by the voice of the teacher, I drifted off into the meditation, quietly becoming aware of my breathing. Slowly, gently, I felt a wave of calmness wash over me, a warmth that carried with it a feeling of love of self, and peace. I felt so open.

Being open is to acknowledge whatever rises into consciousness without reacting to it and having full acceptance of whatever the present moment has to offer. For me, this state of being leads to the most productive meditation session. I was allowing my walls to come down, letting thoughts flow in and out of my conscious mind. This gave me a chance to look at things in a different way, through a different lens. I soon realized with the practice of meditation peace and calm could be found while doing many things. One day as I was sitting on the rocks, I closed my eyes and was reminded of beautiful, warm summer days sitting on the waters' edge and listening to the seagulls. I realized I had been doing this when I was a child! During these times of meditation, I found myself closer to God, perhaps the closest I've ever felt to Him.

My curiosity peaked! I wanted to learn and know more. I started reading a lot of books about spirituality and was especially drawn to Deepak Chopra. I liked he was a doctor and connected your physical body with your spiritual essence. The book I really connected with most was "The Healing Self". He spoke about cleaner eating, environmental toxins, and so much more. It helped me with the challenges I faced as I attempted to make these specific changes in my lifestyle. His writings on the mind-body connection resonated deeply with me. He spoke a lot about the positive effects of meditation and healing. I was fascinated with intuition; those little whispers one gets, gently nudging them in a certain direction or away from a bad situation. My intuition was strong. I began to realize it had been all along. Sensing people's emotions even before they spoke could sometimes be an eye-opening experience. My premonitions were becoming stronger as well. Sometimes I had visions or thoughts of things before they happened. Here is an example of what I am speaking of. One night my daughter went to a concert. When she left, I had this unsettling feeling, a sort of "bad vibe", which proved itself to come true. Afterwards, I started to wonder if I made it happen or was it only a feeling because of my connection with my daughter.

I discovered I could tell when someone wasn't being truthful with me. I get this 'vibe' as I like to call it, a certain way my body feels when they speak to me and aren't telling the truth. I also pay attention to see if they are making eye contact with me. It's a bullshit radar; I can feel it and there are times it actually makes me sick.

Added to all the other sensations and feelings, there was always the feeling of spirit around me. It started when I would walk into a room and not feel "alone". I began sensing or seeing something out of the corner of my eye. Sometimes I would smell a familiar perfume or after-shave or feel a presence near me. I was never afraid of the sensations. In fact, I felt very comforted by these random visits. I started to notice little things and pay attention to "signs". Have you ever walked to your car and saw a coin next to your door or have other items just appear? Random things like that happen to me all the time. Cardinals pay me a special visit sometimes, on days when it seems I need it the most. I also see numbers everywhere, on clocks, license plates, etc.... Numbers like 111. 911, 1313, 77. Maybe you have had similar experiences?

Journaling became a favorite way to write about my experiences, so I was able to refer to them later. It also became a way to learn more about myself and how I was developing my skills. I was feeling at home with my new spiritual practices. I was more in touch with myself and God than I'd ever been before. For me, this confirmed I was exactly where I needed to be. I felt a sense of relief I had finally found a place where I belonged. These new experiences also brought so many new and interesting people into my life; like-minded people who had the same questions I did about life. Sometimes life challenges force you to dig deeper and face the things you were avoiding. I wasn't a bad person; I wasn't looking to get into trouble; I was lost and now I found myself.

Allowing myself to explore and look for answers to questions I'd had for a long time, opened doors , putting people in my path I could learn from. Finding the answers, I had been seeking, I realized the doors and opportunities were opening right before me.

I was starting to see myself for who I was becoming – inquisitive and trusting more in my intuitive self. It did become apparent I had no boundaries and began to understand how the lack of safe personal space was contributing to my health issues and constant state of stress. Now I could see why my constant overflow of emotions had gotten the better of me. I was an Empath.

For many years, I had suffered with chronic pain and autoimmune illnesses. Western medicine wasn't helping. I felt a lot of frustration and hopelessness. I was tired of the nasty side effects of the new medicines. I was quickly losing hope of ever feeling better again.

My intuition told me to try a different approach. I decided to investigate alternative treatments which included Reiki. Up until this point, I had never heard of this spiritual practice. My new network of friends included Reiki practitioners. Reiki (also called Universal Life Energy) is a beautiful healing modality. It moves energy thought the practitioner, encouraging emotional and physical healing to the patient. I was eager for my first session. It was an emotional experience for me. My body felt relaxed, my mind calm. As a result of the session, wanting to take a Reiki course was a no-brainer! If I could learn the healing techniques and make someone else feel the way I did afterwards, I was going to do it.

Things were really aligning for me. The Universe was guiding and pushing me in the direction I needed to go, not only for myself, to also help others. For me, giving Reiki to someone was as healing as it was receiving. There was so much new information flooding in, so many new things I wanted to explore. Wanting to learn as much as I could about everything I was discovering; I became a sponge. Attending workshops, classes, and conferences, all of it was exciting. I couldn't get enough! It made me feel like I was connecting to something bigger than myself.

Although so much had happened in my life, this was the true beginning of my journey, my healing journey. I was discovering who I truly was – an Empath, a healer, an intuitive, a spiritualist. This was what the Universe had planned for me. My soul was starting to feel at peace and more things were making sense, Things like why I was the way I was as a child. I was a sensitive, not just a quirky, nerdy girl. I was an empath! I wasn't crazy!

In the beginning, I was uncomfortable talking about my newfound gifts to most people. I was afraid of being judged. Or perhaps I was the one judging them. Inside I was fearful they would not understand and wouldn't accept me. Yet, how could I be embarrassed by something that felt wonderful and made me so happy?

So, I kept quiet. Other than my "spiritual friends," I didn't speak about my new experiences. What was I really learning here? Why was I holding back? It was my Ego holding me back, not trusting myself enough to let go of fear.

Why are some people more connected or "tuned in" than others? Why is it we often don't learn from these simple things which can make us feel so connected? Sometimes, the daily stresses of life, past and present traumas, and anxieties can cloud our visions and keep us from seeing our truths. We can miss the "signs", the intuitive whispers and those all too familiar "gut" feelings. Why don't we trust them? What makes us finally wake up?

For me it was a series of events that shook me to the core, my wake-up call to trust myself. Something near and dear to my own personal life, something that couldn't possibly happen to me. I had been ignoring the signs and my own symptoms. I ignored the dreams I was having of certain things going to happen. Happen they did. It was then I realized this was something I had to pay attention to. I would no longer ignore it. Now, I acknowledge everything I feel. If I had paid attention to the signs, the dreams sooner, I may have been able to prevent a serious situation. From this I learned once you let go, and allow yourself to receive, the possibilities are endless. Why are people so scared to take this journey?

This began yet another journey, my spiritual awakening. I had heard this term used so many times. It sounded so mystical and beautiful, like waking up one day and suddenly knowing all the answers, reaching total enlightenment. Doesn't that sound about right? The truth is, it's not anything like that at all. A spiritual awakening can be raw, ugly, and painful. It can take years and will walk you through your darkest times. It's a roller coaster of emotions, life changes and experiences. Through the process, you begin to realize every single thing you experienced, had its reason. It can be a massive test of your faith requiring total blind trust. A spiritual awakening means taking steps without knowing where your feet are going to land. This is what it's really like to go through a spiritual awakening. Most often we don't know what's happening until we are halfway through it. Then we understand all the signs that lead up to it and we finally start paying attention. One day, in the midst of the struggle, something dawns on you, this spiritual awakening is what is happening. Yet, some don't realize or acknowledge it. I feel an awakening is a gift. My heart hurts when for those who don't acknowledge it. Most will continue to have a hard time in life, lose jobs, go through bad relationships and more; all signs they are ignoring it's time to make needed changes in their lives.

Why would anyone choose to go through something so painful? Most of us want to understand ourselves on a deeper level, to reach our full potential, to know what a peaceful life feels like. This desire to know develops into the search for something bigger than ourselves. It requires letting go of the things that hold us back. For me, it about being kind to those who made it difficult to do so, having a clear conscious, and knowing I was living my best life with a connection to my higher power. I wanted to feel the wholeness, the ultimate connection to myself and develop the understanding all things happen for a reason. These are the reasons why those of us who choose to walk through fire, go through what we do.

Thanks to all I have learned and experienced, I have come to the point where I am grateful. This gratitude provides me a feeling of happiness I haven't experienced previously ; the feeling of life events coming full circle. Even though things may not have always gone the way I hoped, I have so much to be grateful for. I am finally at peace with myself and feel like everything has fallen into place. I have met my tribe, who are a unique, eclectic bunch. I have been blessed with wonderful clients to work with. I can honestly say I love the work I do. Reiki is something my clients love. It improves their mood, helps with sleep and has been such a blessing for me to connect with them on this deeper level.

My spiritual work, educating people, working with healing crystals, readings, Reiki, and writing help make my life complete. I am always growing and still love to learn. I continue to take advantage of opportunities placed in front of me. Life is about lessons and I have learned many. One of the most important is PAY ATTENTION TO YOUR GUT!

I'm still the little girl in the woods in a lot of ways. My love for music, nature, art, and animals hasn't changed at all. I lovingly embrace my quirky personality. I still love my alone time and have an active imagination. I still sit at the water's edge, making drip castles. You see, the child in us is always there. It is important to connect to your inner child, for they hold lessons we can learn from them. Having the spark of your inner child within, brings you joy as an adult. Like now, playing the guitar and getting back to music excites me. These things connect me with my inner child, and

I understand I was too young to see the relevance of all I was, including being an empath. It has changed my perspective of who I was as a child. Life has come full circle.

"If you're always
trying to be normal
you will never
know how amazing
you can be!"

Maya Angelou

Stan was born in Detroit but claims Albion, Michigan as his home. He has been employed in the Information Technology field for over 25 years and is an Assistant Vice-President with a US-based multinational financial services company.

He has received several Volunteer of the Year Awards in his local market for his engagement and activism with youth as well as the Starr Commonwealth Distinguished Alumni Award. Stan owned and operated Transition Bodyworks for over 13 years as a Usui Reiki Master (Japanese Healing Art) and Massage Therapy practitioner.

He currently serves as vice-chairman of the Starr Commonwealth Board of Trustees, and has served in other officer positions on the Board. He is also President and Committee Chairman of the Starr Alumni Association. Stan has received the Albion High School Distinguished Alumni Award and is a member of the committee. One of his favorite memories is holding the high school shotput record established in 1974, which still stands today.

Stan and his wife Patricia live in the Midwest. He enjoys camping, motorcycle riding and kite flying.

Contact Stanley at transition_bodyworks@juno.com

STANLEY E. ALLEN

Usui Reiki Master, Massage Therapy practitioner,
Distinguished Youth Services Volunteer

Why Not Me?

I'm sitting here on this winter Sunday, looking out my sunroom windows thinking about how blessed I am to be able to be here, in this place, living a life of comfort, healing, compassion and forgiveness. As I've gotten older, I've come to realize that life is a very precious commodity and should be experienced to its fullest. But this was not always the case. There were times in life when I didn't think it mattered if I lived or died. My very existence was a big question mark early in life. Why me? Why am I here and what purpose do I serve? Only by the grace of God and the healing opportunities I've experienced along this journey have I found the answers to those questions and much more.

I am often reminded that I am no longer that young man who grew up in Detroit, Michigan. The one that had done some things, some bad things, which I now consider to be mistakes-turned-into-healing-opportunities in life. Seeking approval, I was trying to find my place in an effort to be somebody that mattered when I grew up. I was a foster child living a scary, transient life. A life where you try to fit in, doing anything to simply belong.

A month before my fifth birthday, my mother died. Getting through her death was tough, really tough. As a small child, I didn't understand why she had to die, or what death even was for that matter. All I knew is that I felt suddenly abandoned by the only person I'd ever loved and who'd ever loved me. I was dependent on her for my happiness, my well-being, feelings of being nurtured and all of that was gone in an instant. They took Mom away in an ambulance as I stood watching on the street corner, and there was no way I could comprehend this at all. The next thing I remember is looking at her laying in a casket at the funeral. I'll always remember the turquoise dress and silver earrings she wore. I have memories of someone trying to lift me up to see her as I was kicking and screaming, terrified of her lying there motionless and cold. I was crying and couldn't understand why she wouldn't wake up. The sudden feeling of detachment from her was overwhelming. Little did I know then what an impact this would have on me for the rest of my life and the work I would eventually do to help others.

After my mother's death I became a ward of the state. My brother and I were placed at the Wayne County Juvenile Hall until an uncle came and took us to live with him. He was an extreme disciplinarian who believed that boys had to have their spirits broken. How could he think our spirits weren't already broken? He would tie us to a chair and beat us with a lead-filled rubber hose, one that he personally crafted especially for the occasion. In this day and age this would most definitely be considered child abuse and there would have been repercussions for his actions. My brother ran away soon after the beatings began, leaving me to endure the almost daily beatings alone. For years after, I thought my brother leaving was my fault. Forty years later we would be reunited. He told me he was sorry he'd left me there alone to take his 'share' of the beatings, but said he just couldn't stay any longer. Eventually I forgave him for also abandoning me. It wasn't an easy thing to do, that's for sure, but I thank God for every moment we were able to spend as brothers until his death.

Teachers at school began to question me about bruises and welts that were never completely hidden by my long sleeve shirts. This was the only reason the beatings stopped. The social worker assigned to my case was informed by the school and I was removed from my uncle's care. As a result, I ended up in the Wayne County Juvenile Hall again. Saying I had become a bitter young man was an understatement. I was totally unapproachable and acquired labels such as incorrigible and anti-social. I remember standing in my cell, looking out through the screened windows from the 4th floor and asking "Why? Why am I here? Why doesn't someone come pick me up?"

Every time a voice came over the loudspeaker telling a kid to "roll up" I would anxiously wait for my name to be called. Almost two years later, it was finally my time. WOW!! I couldn't believe it. I felt a surge of relief. Someone was finally coming to get me. My aunt, father and grandmother were there waiting for me, ready to take me to live with them. Even though my father, along with his wife and 6 kids, lived in the flat upstairs, he never played much of a part in my life. He worked nights, sleeping during the day. I never really saw him much. When he did have time, it was already taken by his other family. This hurt deeply. As a result, I would hold on more dearly to the love of my grandmother.

My grandmother ended up being the greatest influence on me at this time of my life. I remember her warm, soft hands and her gentle hazel eyes. She helped me build a strong character and taught me about modesty. She taught me how to cook and sew. I have fond memories of making a couple of quilts with her. Through her I came to know God. She always made sure we went to church every Sunday. Her touch was always so soft and warm it would make me melt. She was the first person I can honestly say I loved.

We lived on the east side of Detroit and it wasn't too long before I was ditching school and hanging out with the older guys at the neighborhood pool hall. We used to give a kid 25 cents a bottle to bring us Boones Farm apple wine out of the back of this Greek grocery store. When we didn't have money to buy it, we took it. We considered ourselves pretty much unstoppable, doing what we wanted when we wanted. At the age of fourteen I had become a member of the Jr. Black Avengers. The gang made me feel like I was part of something bigger; it filled that need for something to belong to, something which was lacking in my life. Reflecting on this time,

I realize now I was looking for a brother or a tribe, anything to make me feel wanted, to make me feel like I belonged. Getting into fights became an outlet, a sort of relief that I found myself welcoming because it allowed me to vent my anger. I was good at it. The release felt good too.

During Junior High my life took yet another turn. It was during this time my grandmother became ill with what we now know as Alzheimer's and gradually she forgot me. It was devastating to hear her ask me, "Where's Stanley?" The one person I knew who loved me more than anyone didn't recognize me anymore. Once again, I couldn't believe this was happening nor did I understand why. If only someone had helped explain this to me perhaps the process of this loss would have helped me. I lost my grandmothers guidance and, I thought, her love, all of which I had taken for granted. I've wished so many times later in life that I had listened and paid more attention when she tried to get me to do the right thing.

With my grandmother's failing health my desire to hang out with the gang increased. I was remanded once again to Wayne County Juvenile Hall, my third trip there in eleven years. Being a ward of the state no longer mattered to me. I was angry, hurt and just didn't care what happened to me anymore. Why shouldn't I just give up? After spending some significant time in the juvenile hall, my social worker and a big burley guy took me to a place called Starr Commonwealth.

Starr Commonwealth, founded in 1913 under the premise "There is no such thing as a bad child" was now home. I was a student there from 1970 to 1974. In the beginning I just went through the motions; going to class every day, working out in the gym. As time went on, I got involved in sports, playing football and participating in shotput. Shotput is a track and field sport where athletes try to "put" a heavy, weighted ball as far as they can, without throwing it. The shotput has been part of the Olympics since 1896. I discovered I was good at sports and took every opportunity to be involved. This made me feel like I finally had abilities at something. I also worked on one of the co-op farms, learning how to milk cows and bale hay, earning a quarter an hour. Little did I know how much things were about to change for the better. I was placed in a program with some other young men and now had an opportunity to attend the local high school.

I was a pretty athletic guy back then - 6'2, 250 lbs. and could move pretty quick. At Albion High

School I played football for the Wildcats and threw the shotput in track. Once a Wildcat, always a Wildcat! One of the first awkward experiences of high school came when I tried out for the football team. One day I was in the locker room when this white kid and Italian kid came up to me. The white kid said, "Are you one of those convicts from Starr?" I turned around to look at him, ready to punch him because I was so angry. Who is he to call me a convict? He just looked at me. There was something about the way he looked at me when he said it. Instead of listening to his words, I looked in his eyes, then realized he was smiling at me. Oddly enough, there was a connection there and an acceptance. He became my best friend. I'll never forget the shocking comment but at the same time his acceptance of this "convict."

Before too long his family became my family. His parents embraced me as one of their own although they already had several kids. It was the first time I really experienced what I thought family life was supposed to be and I will always be grateful. It helped me, at least for a couple years, feel like a member of a family I always felt like I should have had. There was such a sense of belonging, to a degree that I'd never experienced before. It was a piece I needed, the connection and acceptance of others. I didn't realize when I was at Starr and going to Albion High School that it would all have such an impact on my life. It really helped mold the person I've become today.

It was also during my time at Albion High School that I met my "chosen" mom. There she was, this woman with curly hair who always wore athletic outfits and always had clean tennis shoes. God saw fit to put her in my life. She was the school's gym teacher, and everyone loved her. She was always there to listen to us kids; she cared about all of the kids and let us know it. At the same time, she was also truthful and told us when we messed up. I really respected her and loved her smile and laughter.

I remember the day she asked me, "What's the matter? Is something wrong?" as I was walking down the hall with a really bad attitude. You know the kind where you have that walk, that face and that energy that says stay away from me? As I walked away from her she told me, "Don't walk away." I was having a bad day and it must have been apparent that my attitude sucked. I didn't want to talk to her, but it was obvious she wasn't going to let me leave until I told her what was going on. This was our first real encounter and it was the first time in a long time I had a feeling that someone cared. She is a strong, caring woman and like my grandmother, she was a positive role model for me. She became my mentor and even today she is the matriarch in the community; someone who believes it takes a village to raise the children. She showed me unconditional love and made me feel like somebody cared about me as a person.

Over time, we became very close and the topic of possible adoption came up. At first, we would joke about it but I never thought she was serious. One day after school she took me to her house to introduce me to her husband. I remember how he looked at me – remember I'm 6'2" and 250lbs. He looked at her, then they both looked at me. It was that look like, "Seriously? Are you kidding me?" Another awkward moment in time. Maybe I didn't really believe it would happen. The thought of adoption swiftly evaporated. There was never a reason given why the adoption didn't happen and I didn't ask, primarily because I really didn't want to know. I was afraid I wasn't good enough or that I had done something wrong. It was just one more disappointment to endure which I had no control over. To this day I still don't know why she didn't adopt me, but it's not important. In my healing process over the years, I've come to understand that the reasons why something did or didn't happen is not as important as the lessons to be learned from the experiences themselves.

It's taken me several years to understand and appreciate all the lessons I learned from this amazing woman. I am filled with nothing but gratitude now for all that she taught me. She was, and is, a wonderful example of kindness, compassion and love which God put in my life back then, and who remains to guide me to this day as my mentor.

In high school, I remember feeling that even though there were all these people around me who seemingly cared, I was still a lone wolf. There was no sense of permanency; I was always waiting for the next big move in my life to occur. I guess you can say I was very insecure. This often meant not getting too close to someone, including my chosen mom and my best friend, so the pain or disappointment of leaving wouldn't be so great. I started masking my feelings so others wouldn't see my pain, trying to make myself numb to the pain of separation. Taking solace in being alone, I created a pretty solid barrier around myself in order to protect my heart. I wasn't going to depend on anyone for anything, EVER! I decided that I was going to take care of myself and never rely on others for my happiness or fulfillment. Little did I know at the time, how far off the mark my thinking was.

After "aging out" of Starr and graduating from high school, I attempted college. College wasn't exactly for me so I went into military service in the Navy. I thought it would be an opportunity to serve and what better thing to do than serve your country. After the service, I continued to feel a desire to make a difference. Regardless of how often I tried to ignore it, I am grateful this feeling never left me. I found myself aligning with service-oriented projects in life, including working with developmentally disabled adults. During this part of my life, I came to realize I have a great ability to be compassionate and empathetic.

When I look at what kids are dealing with today, I feel like it's my calling as someone who has "made it through" to give them compassion and support. I am blessed, by the grace of God, to be able to use my own spiritual enlightenment and healing to help a person feel better about themselves or their situation. Through listening and communicating I can help someone realize they aren't the only one who's gone through rough times, and that they can make things better. My high school mentor taught me that regardless of how bad or good it gets, the important thing is to not let it stop you from trying to succeed and make something positive of your life.

The art of forgiveness is one of the most powerful lessons I learned in my discoveries of life. I've learned that by opening yourself up and allowing God into your life, you can obtain a measure of forgiveness far beyond your own expectations. Being a Lone Wolf can be so detrimental to spiritual, psychological and emotional well-being. You can't begin to grasp and understand what you need to learn by shutting everything or everyone out. Dare I say it's not about religion? It's about connection with God. It's about that spiritual connection which resonates within our chests and our hearts.

In the process of my healing I have learned to forgive myself for making bad decisions and mistakes, while also being accountable and responsible for having made them. I've learned that you don't necessarily have to be born into a family to find a family. In my healing process I've become more aware and inviting of support. I've realized I can't do it alone. Unfortunately, these types of circumstances are faced by people every single day. I feel fortunate to have learned enough through living, loving and healing to diminish the scars of trauma I carried for so many years

In my opinion, ownership and self-forgiveness are the first critical steps in the healing process. Once you forgive yourself for mistakes you've made, the forgiveness of others comes almost automatically and is much easier to obtain. It's no easy task to allow yourself the ability to forgive, to try to look for the positive things and not dwell on the negative.

Back in 2003, I returned to Starr Commonwealth and Albion for the first time in almost 30 years. I was unprepared for the memories and feelings it brought back to me. I've often said if not for Starr Commonwealth I'd be dead. I've also gone back to Detroit and what was a once beautiful neighborhood from my childhood is now burned out. Old friends are in jail, prison, dead or hooked on something, or away in mental facilities. Detroit is rebuilding but it will never be what it once was in my young mind's eye.

I believe there needs to be more places like Starr Commonwealth for our youth to heal and discover their potential. Even though I didn't take advantage of all the opportunities then, Starr is more special to me as an adult. I've now found my purpose and my tribe in the process and became comfortable in my own skin. I've learned over the years that being a lone wolf was not all it's cracked up to be. It's lonely!

I've volunteered my time, my talent and my treasure to the youth of Starr over the years. No longer am I a Lone Wolf in my heart or mind. People need people in order to survive. I have learned the importance of being connected to others, that it is actually very beneficial in more ways than one. This place is a part of my life; it's a part of me and who I've become as an adult. It helped me, increased my survival rate substantially and indeed assisted me in finding my purpose.

Every time I see the young men and women walking around campus on their way to class, I can't help but hope they grasp the opportunities provided to them; to find out who they are, to learn something new and different spiritually while establishing relationships. I feel a great sense of empathy and compassion towards them because my heart relates. I have such an in-depth understanding of what life is like for them and what they're going through; the uncertainty and distrust not just for authority but people in general, the need to find seclusion in one's own mind and heart because of the distrust which has manifested between them and the world around them. The Lone Wolf believes it is safer to be alone. Safer than extending themselves and trusting someone else because the disappointment is so great, the hurt beyond imagination when that trust is broken. I ache for those who are not taking full advantage of the opportunities placed before them because that's what I did when I was there as a student. I know what it's like to feel as though my existence doesn't matter and that sense of waiting to see what's going to happen next. Not knowing if it's going to get better or worse, always expecting more of the same.

If I could give advice and touch each of their hearts, I would say, "Please take the opportunities placed before you right now. It will help you reset and find out who you are in this world, not just who others think you are or should be. This is an opportunity to learn something truly amazing about yourself by establishing relationships and connecting with others." I am known as "Uncle Stan" on campus nowadays, which feels humbling and amazing. I get to share with these awesome kids that instead of what is consuming your mind, ask yourself how you can get the most out of this experience.

I feel it's important for us as adults to try to foster healing and promote resiliency in today's kids. We should encourage them not to give up, to find ways to show care and compassion, to assist them with a hand up. Young people nowadays don't have the coping skills to understand what's going on around them. They find the easy way and check out emotionally with drugs. Some of them check out permanently, never knowing what life as an adult could have been like. It saddens me they will never know or realize their true worth, or their value to reach their fullest potential.

When I am on campus and walking through the buildings at Starr, there are paintings, pictures, plaques and awards representing its history. It reminds me of those who have come before me and how far I have come as a person. When I walked these halls as a kid, not knowing what would happen next, I never imagined I would be here again, able to inspire and assist young people and to be treated with respect and admiration. I absolutely never saw this as part of my life when I was living in anger and fear. My purpose is to share the honesty as well, like my mentor did with me. Because only when you're honest can you start the healing process for self or assist others.

A firm spiritual connection with God today drives and compels me to be an example for those who are feeling alone. I want to tell them to look within, to have a conversation with God and they will find some answers. God gave us an opportunity to be here and it's up to us to accept and make the most of it. I've come to realize the importance of leaving a legacy. I want my existence on Mother Earth to be about more than just my own personal journey. Having come from nothing, it's important for me to leave something of value that will benefit others. Now it is my redemption and my mission to serve. It's a big part of my motivation for sharing my story.

We have a responsibility and accountability for the development of our children. The ability for us, the parent, to listen and learn how to communicate are essential to our existence, in my opinion. Without this it would be hard pressed to survive and thrive in this world and reach our fullest potentiality as adults. To be effective there has to be some 'give and take' in each relationship.

It's our responsibility to ensure our children have the chance to develop self-esteem, courage, resiliency and provide the opportunity to thrive. Some are born into it while others must create it. I have found my purpose and I am leaning into it more every day. I believe that God put me here to be an example for others. It's become important to me to help young adults understand that even if they feel alone, God is with them. There will be opportunities to flourish, thrive and most importantly heal if they look closely within. I want to tell others to continue to believe in themselves, find their connection spiritually with God, and serve a higher purpose as a child of God. To trust that regardless of what happens, when it is all said and done, God HAS a purpose for you. Take comfort that God is within each and every one of us.

The message I want to leave is this: We have a very short time here on this earth. I used to ask, "Why Me?" Now I ask, "Why Not Me?" We should all strive to find compassion and love for one another as God intended us to do.

Messages from the Angels

Pathway to Awakening

Channeled through Deborah Finley
Medium, Author
Women Standing Strong Together

Dear Ones, we love you so much.

Call upon us, your Angels, as we were created to help you in the highest possible ways.

The pathway to awakening is different for everyone, for some the pathway has been long, and for others it is not so. All are born with the gift of free will, with the voice of one's higher-self inside. The knowing resides within. You have the power all along, the choice is always yours.

Awaken the voice of your Soul! Remember who you are… for you are a child of God, the Creator.

The higher vibrational light energy is there for you! This higher frequency will continue to raise your vibration. This all-powerful light is above you, below you and all around you.

Fill yourselves up, ignite the flame within you, then send it outward into the world to reach all those who seek it as you once did.

Be the channel for the messages of hope, for today hope is needed more than ever. Encourage the people to choose Love, the energy of compassion, and you will experience God's grace, all those who choose this path will be awakened.

Remember free will, honor the choices made. Some will sleep, will choose hate, selfishness, greed. They are unhappy by choice. All already know and understand; the choices they make will reawaken them or further deepen their sleep. Until they have had enough of going against what the wisdom of the soul tells them, for the soul knows, they will sleep. Show them love, compassion and a better way despite them.

You were born in the energy of love, of intelligence. It is time to live in the present, time for self-love. This is your time, that brings forth an opportunity to continue to radiate at the higher vibrational light frequency.

For you, dear ones, were born with an awareness, born awake. Sometimes you have strayed and walked, sleeping, in the past. However, the unrest within called you back. Your Soul knew better.

For we, God's Angels, gently nudged you along. Trusting in this guidance will never lead you wrong. For you are the helpers on the earth realm; the healers, the mediums, comforters, and teachers.

Honor the Creator, and your fellow humankind, by allowing all the access to be shown by example, the pathway to awakening. We are God's loving helpers, the comforters, the protectors and guardians. We are with you now and always.

"I know this
transformation is painful,
but you're not falling
apart; You're just falling
into something different,
with a new capacity
to be beautiful."

- William C. Hannan

Julie Shackelford resides in Tucson, Arizona. Active hiker, walker, and biker she loves communing with Nature.

Julie is a lightworker and Empath as well as an Art Intuitive Life coach. She is also a musician, an Award Winning watercolor artist, author and speaker. Mother of 5 children (2 autistic boys) and advocate for Autism awareness. Her spouse spent 14 years in the United States Army so she is also a former Army wife and is no stranger to moving all over the world. A certified teacher in the Law Of Attraction, Julie loves to co-create with clients to live the life they have always dreamed of.

Reach Julie at Hodgepodgejulie@yahoo.com

Acuity scheduling link:
        https://hodgepodgejulie.as.me/

Facebook business page: Hodgepodgejulie

JULIE
SHACKELFORD

Lightworker, Empath,
Art Intuitive Life Coach, Author, Speaker

To my magical daughter Emily Ruth - who's favorite color is the rainbow. May you always shine in colors.

Original Artwork © Julie Shackelford

Ask and It Is Given

Slowly, my ears began to focus on the alarm and my eyes fluttered open. I can remember thinking to myself, "No, not again, not another day." How can a good Christian woman, following all the rules, feel so depressed? "Live your life without sin and you will be rewarded." Those words echoed in my mind. I had no idea what else was 'out there.' This was all I knew at the time.

The day would come when I was considering different options. Standing in front of the mirror at the medicine cabinet, I wanted the suffering to be over. Peering over to the bathtub, I thought if I slit my wrists and let the blood ooze out until there was no breath left inside of me, I would not have to take one more step into this dull, disappointing and crazy life of mine. A sudden realization flooded through me. My kids, OMG, how difficult would it be for them to find their mother lying on the bathroom floor, breathless? Surely there was another way?

The medicine cabinet held the secret, the answer was right before me. That brown bottle, the one we kept hidden for times we needed some pain relief, that prescription drug was staring back at me saying, "Yes, I am the solution." If I just take them all now, I could end this life! Just then, divine intervention happened, I believe. A feeling rushed through me when suddenly, I thought, "There must be something more in this lifetime than being miserable." After all, I had children, a husband who supported us and a beautiful home. How could I be so miserable all the time? All I could think about was my kids and how difficult this would be for them as tears began to flow, so I decided suicide was not the answer. These amazing and beautiful angels actually saved my life because they were all home on this day. Yes, God put angels in my life and now I knew I had to shift my perspective. All these scriptures I learned had to have a deeper meaning for me. There must be something hidden that could lift this depression.

Depression can kick in anytime; like a shadow creeping up behind you and BAM! It wasn't as if there was a moment, a day, or a time where I thought consciously to myself, "Hey Julie, something is terribly wrong here."

Can you imagine living in a prison within your own mind? The darkness that encompassed my thoughts was spreading into my cells, squeezing the life out of me. Wandering thoughts floated in daily, "Why do I have to live?"

Each day, I felt suffocated by the thought of all my daily tasks that were expected of me. It was formidable and unfulfilling. Nothing was creative in my life and I needed something more if I was going to truly live.

My faith was all I knew at this point; at least the faith I knew from the church and my upbringing as a daughter of a Methodist Minister. Growing up in this environment made me feel trapped, judged and shamed. Whatever I did, whatever I wore, everything was a judgement back onto my father, the minister.

I could remember, as I knelt in church one day, thinking about all my expectations. How could I feel such shame, guilt and judgement as a Christian mom? How can I be so disgruntled with my life? There was no one for me to share my story with. I felt desperately alone and angry. I knew this would become toxic and these emotions were not healthy or proactive. I had to be honest with my feelings first and learn how to express them in my relationships.

I didn't feel like I could reach out to my husband who already had his own pressures of financially supporting our family and discipling our children. I didn't want to add any more onto his shoulders. The martyr came out as I took this journey, to walk it alone. I had to figure out a way to shift my behaviors and start working on myself by accepting responsibility. But how and where?

I felt judged when I reached out to my community, especially the women. They had no empathy or sympathy for me, at least that is how I felt. They just kept telling me I should pray more, which wasn't working. It was really about me loving myself and accepting the fact that 'what was considered perfect' is just an opinion. I had to learn how to express my hurt feelings because resentments were cropping up everywhere.

Then that day came, the one where I felt so embarrassed and ashamed. The uncontrollable tears, anger and shaking washed over me when I got that 'look' one more time because my autistic son had a meltdown in church. You would think someone would say, "May I help you with your son?" Instead, I just felt horrible. Did they have any idea how it felt when they pointed and whispered amongst themselves?

The dreaded and inevitable sermon made me feel worse when our minister would speak to us about discipline. Where is the compassion and fellowship in this Christian community? Do they not understand my child is not spoiled, but gifted and trying to fit into this judgmental world?

Where is my God? In this moment, I could not understand what I was expected to do anymore. Feeling abandoned by my loving God, I just wanted to run away at that moment. No longer did I want to be a slave to the depression or the old indoctrinations I was perceiving, that felt so limiting. God, please help me.

Where had the magic gone in life where I was the star of my day, having fun, laughing and feeling my connection with God?

I found myself reflecting upon a time from my childhood where I could see myself rubbing my hand on the headboard in my room and tracing the golden leaves. These were special times when I felt like a princess. Growing up in Missouri, I remember a time sitting on the swing in the park as the sun washed over my face and I had a sense of unlimited freedom. I wanted this freedom once again! I wanted to stop worrying about others who I felt were judging me. I desired to be in alignment with my true self, my passion, so my spirit would shine once again.

Little did I realize how much fantasy ideas would play in my life. June Cleaver was just one of the perfect TV Mom role-models I watched when I was ten years old. The show, *Leave it to Beaver*, where she starred as the 'perfect' everything, was a Hollywood portrayal of the impossible. It's no wonder I went crazy. Her romantic portrayal of life as a wife and mom made it look so easy. Now, looking back, there was nothing romantic about any of it. Talk about a Hollywood fantasy!

I was such a HOT mess! Perfectly engaged in home schooling and preparing dinner, I wondered how could I ever be 'perfect' when my husband arrived home after a busy day. Are these fantasies applying pressure on us, making us feel less than worthy? Who has time for makeup when you are taking care of 2 autistic children and 3 other kids? The more I attempted to look and be like the perfect TV wife, the more challenges I created for myself, the less resilient I became.

While I was doing my best to dress up and welcome my husband home from a long day at work, the kids were emptying the baby powder on the floor. By the time my husband got home, I was a train wreck! You know, hair frazzled, no pretty dress, sometimes barely put together at all and often exhausted. It felt like a never-ending cycle.

I was taught in the Bible to study and learn how to be the best Christian woman I could be. If I continued to read my bible every day and memorize scripture, then I would be given some divine help or inspiration. But Saint Julie I was never going to be no matter how hard I tried. Not even close! This Julie needed a renewed sense of connection, fast!

I began searching for a place, a home where I could fit in. It became a daunting and endless task seeking some 'building or church' to find my connection. It was so close, I just needed to live in the present moment to see it. Perhaps a mindset shift was all I needed to rid myself of the negativity. That's it! I will ask for help.

I found myself kneeling before the priest at

confession one Sunday, opening my heart and soul, reaching for a lifeline. As I began to express my hopelessness, the priest's words echoed in my mind, "Julie this is your cross to bear."

"No," I thought to myself, "I don't want to carry this big wooden cross that is breaking my back and my heart."

Oh, how I ached for some relief. There just had to be more to my life! I stood up to leave confessional that day determined not to be a victim any longer. I would find a way!

I got angry! Why wasn't I happy? There had to be more to this world than feeling like a victim. I was done. Anger was boiling in my stomach. I pondered for a moment, how do these other women do this and are they really happy inside?

There it was, believe it or not, an answer on social media. Sheesh, God has a funny way of showing up in this technological world!

Money boot camp! What was that? I needed more money! Would that really make me happy and solve my problems?

Was it a scam? It sounded almost too good to be true, but I kept thinking what if this is it? What if this could be the key to helping me improve my finances and start improving my life? Something started to stir inside of me again. What if it did work, I asked myself. Allowing myself to think 'what if' had not happened in a very long time. I had a small ray of hope and dreams began to shine upon me inside. So, I signed up!

Interestingly, a bible verse was the name of the book I had to purchase, *"Ask and It Shall Be Given, Learning to Manifest Your Dreams"* by Esther and Jerry Hicks. That Bible verse was *"Ask and it will be given to you, seek and you will find; knock and the door will be opened to you"* (Matthew 7:7). Was this the hidden meaning I had been searching for my whole life?

Was the bible teaching me all along? Was my interpretation lost somehow? Why was I not getting it all these years? As I opened the book I felt an immediate shock run through my body. I wrote the date 8/6/2018. My curiosity was peaked! Later, I would realize my soul was talking to me. Deep inside of me, I knew this was something I had been searching for. Had I been mis-interpreting the word of God all these years? Better yet, who was I listening to? I underlined the section in the front of the book which said... *"When you change the way you look at things, the things you look at change"* (Dr. Wayne W Dyer).

It seems money, or lack thereof, was controlling my mind. I wanted a way out and this bootcamp seemed like a way to provide me something valuable, a new perspective. So, I feverishly and diligently took notes. My intent was to soak it all up and become the epitome of freedom and joyfulness.

What I learned through this process was something so valuable it changed my entire perspective. I realize now it was the simple concept of GRATITUDE! Of course, I knew this! How did I forget? Gratitude was the beginning of my spiritual awakening. What was I grateful for? I could not find one thing to feel grateful for in my life at this moment. I sat on this question for a few days.

There was no gratitude in my life. No gratitude for my children, a husband taking care of us and a home to protect us. I didn't even give gratitude for being able to be a stay at home mom. Sheesh! Had I become so damned selfish, disconnected, negative and pitied upon myself, I did not see the gifts before my very own eyes? How many others in this world would be grateful to have a simple roof over their head and someone who cared about them?

As my brain tried to think and my soul sat in silence, it finally came to me... my green hazel eyes, I am grateful for my eyes to see! The flood gates opened as I sat there feeling gratitude. I was thankful for my calves along with my feet so I could walk. Thankful for my hands so I could do tasks, and my fingers that helped me unbutton my slacks. This was the beginning of the changes in my mind and my thoughts began to shift as I realized I had many things to be grateful for in life. No longer was I focusing on all the shit that was going wrong in my life and I had an attitude adjustment. Could it be so simple? Take one day at a time, Julie, be grateful.

Excitedly talking and sharing gratitude with my family, it was making me so happy. Little did I realize, at that moment, it was going to affect all of us.

A short time after having shared these new concepts with my family, I got to play with my autistic son on our trampoline outside. We had a ball, so we tossed it back and forth and played a grateful game. He said, "I am grateful for......." And after a very, very, long pause... he shouted, "The blue sky!" His answer made me giggle for the first time in a long time. This was going to be fun. He threw the ball back to me, "I am grateful for you" I said, and tossed the ball back to him. I remember feeling such joy. My energy began to shift and I felt delighted and happy with the sun shining down on my cheeks just like when I was a little girl on the swing set. It had been so long since I felt this good. I regained a feeling of hope and a sense of new purpose coming. Things were beginning to change. I was transforming and so would those I touch.

One morning, I was in the kitchen pouring my coffee and my autistic son entered the room. His eyes were as big as saucers; he was thinking and talking very clearly. He started listing off all the things he was thankful for and do you know what... in that moment, I believe he was healed. His speech was clear, his focus was amazing, and I understood everything he was saying. Later that day, he slipped back into his autism stupor, I still think about that day. The power of gratitude had reached him on another level in that moment. This concept of focusing on the 'good thoughts' in my life was actually working. It was literally changing the vibration of my life and the lives of those around me. The shift in frequency completely changed the outlook of my day. There was a new sense of wonder and awe in everything around me. It was like I turned on the TV of my own story. The one I could manage and live to bring me a sense of worth.

My courage came one evening in the kitchen when I decided to chat with my husband and share my excitement. There was another way, a better way I felt, to attract the connection to goodness into our lives. I had doubts he wouldn't accept any of it. I was hopeful he would listen and I was mindful of making eye contact, being respectful and open to him being receptive while I spoke with a softer tone in my voice.

I couldn't believe it, a few weeks later, my husband and I sat down to write our bills with gratitude, just like I had been learning. Thanking the Higher Power for the cell phone bill because we had a cell phone and continuing to feel grateful for all the services we had received. Surprise! That was the first time in 25 years we didn't fight. This was momentous for us! It was an absolute miracle. Imagine that?

I immersed myself in studying the Laws of the Universe, and this new money abundance mindset was fascinating. It wasn't just about money that we spend. It was about the value of everything in our lives. There was so much excitement than the façade I once believed on those TV shows!

There are many laws of the Universe; however, for me, starting with the 7 Natural Laws was an exciting place to begin. These laws are fundamental principles based upon our vibrations we as people give out.

"We are always communicating energetically. Before you have spoken a word, your frequency has relayed volumes of information." – Unknown

The 7 Natural Laws of the Universe:
    Law of Vibration
    Law of Relativity
    Law Cause and Effect
    Law of Polarity
    Law of Gestation
    Law of Rhythm
    Law of Transmutation

Learning about these seven principles proved to be something to live by. I could trace these same principles back into the bible. The one that stood out the most was when Jesus manifested food for the masses. Matthew 14:13-21… *"Taking the five loaves and the two fish and looking up to heaven, he gave thanks and broke the loaves"*… 20 *"They all ate and were satisfied, and the disciples picked up twelve basketfuls of broken pieces that were left over."*… 21 *"The number of those who ate was about five thousand men, besides women and children."* This is such a beautiful example of simple gratitude and abundance.

I began learning about manifestation. The idea or concept that we can feel abundance, positive vibrations, thanking the Universe, being grateful, and waiting for it to come true, with Faith. It gave me hope as I began asking the Universe and thanking the Universe for bringing my family an abundance of food.

One day when my family needed more food, I prayed and thanked my higher power for providing. Shortly after this prayer, the doorbell rang. It was my neighbor bringing us 'loaves of bread!' This was the proof I needed to see that manifesting was real and starting off with being grateful raised my vibration. All I had to do was focus and believe and the universe was showing up for me in ways that I never imagined previously.

The most important part of the process? Surrendering, and not worrying about it so I continued to thank the Universe all the time. It was like making a wish, knowing it would come true. Then, at the right moment, voila! It began happening. Ask and it shall be given. Living in the present moment was a new concept for me and it was about to change my entire life. It would take practice and I was so excitedly willing.

Suddenly, everywhere I looked, there was more color in my day. Can you imagine how a simple shower can be so magical when your feelings come alive? Slowly and mindfully, I felt the liquid soap in my hands, kind of slippery and tacky as I rubbed it on my skin. My cells were bubbling over, almost like popped corn and this felt invigorating! How could I have never noticed this before? My skin felt so smooth and sleek. it felt wonderful to open my senses. Once again, I was reminded of the days as a child when I rubbed my hand on the headboard to feel the golden leaves. Could I be waking up to something greater? The magic I had lost as a child was now coming to me once again.

Such a simple concept; good attracts more good. I began to realize, like a magnet, it can also attract more negativity.

Life is really simple and the more I allowed my positive thoughts to take over, the more I remained positive. I was creating a ripple effect everywhere; my family, friends and in the community. In fact, these same positive ripples can encompass the entire planet. Now, the path was clear. I just had to continue to train myself to focus on the abundance and remove the lack mindset.

When my Higher Power saw I was grateful, more was sent my way. The realization came that my Higher Power wanted me to be happy, content and free to spread my happiness on the planet. It was no longer necessary for me to remain stuck in the shame, blame or guilt of these lower vibrational frequencies. I realized this is my freedom from my perceived critical eyes of my church community. It felt like I was the Phoenix who rose again after burning into ashes. This was a new beginning for me and I had no idea where it would lead me, just yet.

These laws became my obsession to bring the goodness into my daily life. Eventually, I celebrated receiving my certificate to teach this work in life. This led me on an amazing journey to become an Art Intuitive Life Coach, author and public speaker.

Now, you may be asking, what is an art intuitive and how did it change my life?

Did you ever finger paint as a kid? Color outside the lines? Express yourself in some creative way?

Art began to give me the freedom to express my

emotions in a safe environment just as I remembered when I was a little girl. Finger-paints could express my anger. I could be messy – not perfect! I began painting trees and feeling my connection to nature became my refuge, my church.

Taking red or orange and maybe even black, I would pour my emotions onto the paper and swirl the colors around releasing my pent up emotions. If I didn't want anyone to find it, all I had to do was throw it away. There would be no evidence in written word. Drawing trees, sketching them, painting them and listening to them became my connection to nature and my Higher Power.

Blues, purples, greens, orange, yellow and red from the rainbow, I would create pictures filled with magic and a sense of joy. There was a vibration I was creating that became almost magical.

Think about it, you look up to heaven for a rainbow and you look down at hell imagining the blazing red flames. Which frequency do you want to resonate in your life?

The more I introduce art to people, whether it's clay or pen and ink, the more healing vibrations come through in this process. Clay is fun because people can actually feel the texture of it between their fingers, molding and creating something into a shape or figure like we are doing in our own life. It gives them a way to process, a place to begin a healing adventure, just like I experienced this beautiful process in my own life. I often tell my clients we can all raise the Earth's vibration, one paint drop at a time. It starts with loving yourself first and being grateful.

Each morning, during my routine and practicing my meditation, I feel connected to the universe, my soul, my source and self, bringing a sense of peace and joy. The vibration of treating myself to self-care told my Higher Power I was important. Then, people around me treated me with that same importance. I am attracting more goodness into my life. Could it be that simple?

Journaling has become a common practice where I write down everything that I am grateful for, like a gratitude rampage, including my prayer. My Spiritual Counsel, the angels and spirit guides were with me in my heart supporting me each day joyfully. Yoga, dance, and walking have all elevated my life and empowered me to create a freaking amazing powerful journey This is available to all of us and you can live a life you dream of as well, it just takes commitment to self along with responsibility for your thoughts and actions.

I invite you to start today by becoming aware of what you are grateful for and taking one small step into a new, victorious life. This will be the biggest leap of faith you can gift yourself. Today my faith is stronger because I have learned to listen more keenly and astutely to nature and my soul. Our higher power wants the best for us, we just need to listen.

There is one more law I must share with you. The Law of Divine Oneness. It is the foundational law, according to which absolutely everything in our universe is interconnected. I now realize 'everything' our words, every choice, desire and belief you have will also have an impact on the world, and on the people in your life. Now, take that in?

I am Julie, perhaps not a saint but definitely an angel who came into your life today to spread some joy upon your day. Remember, the laws of the universe work with you.

"*Life is like*
a box of chocolates.
You never know
what you are
going to get."

Forrest Gump

Born and raised on the west coast, Lisa moved to Pennsylvania with her husband in 2001 and resides with him, their nearly grown daughter and 4-legged friend with a limp, Marlow.

Lisa works part-time in education where she gets paid to be silly with children as they improve their communication skills. Developing inner awareness is one of her hobbies whether participating in yoga, meditation or expressive arts.

Lisa trained in CA with Chris Zydel/Tim Lajoie and graduated from the Wild Heart Teacher Training Program in February, 2019. You can find her facilitating intuitive painting workshops in her studio basement or at local community venues. It is her passion to guide non-artists to connect to their innate creativity and intuition and more deeply to themselves. She has witnessed that the more we understand and love ourselves, the better we understand and love everybody else.

Website: www.feelyourart.com
Email: lisa@feelyourart.com
IG: lisa_hahnlen

LISA
HAHNLEN

Teacher, Intuitive Art Instructor

Original Artwork © Lisa Hahnlen

6

Childhood Gifts

Sinking into the soft cushions of a brown, paisley armchair for the first time, polite introductions were made. The therapist asked, "Why are you here?" A nervous smirk turned one corner of my mouth down while the other corner shifted upwards. I responded, "To unwrap the presents passed onto me as a kid." And with that quip, so began a journey to explore these "childhood gifts" with my eyes open for the first time. I would eventually learn why I didn't trust myself and awaken parts of myself I never knew existed. I will describe these gifts as boxes filled with my indoctrinations, paradigms, and beliefs which were not serving me at my highest potential.

Have you ever received a beautifully wrapped present only to discover what was inside was not what you asked for or expected? That was how life was from me early on. It was like an invisible force field surrounding my life. Things appeared good from the outside, the image I projected to others. On the inside though, the undercurrent of stress and a double dose of multi-generational patterns of addiction, was anything less than perfect. We show the world one part of ourselves, while the secrets are kept inside and behind closed doors. In this case, "closed boxes".

It reminds me of chocolates in a pretty candy box. You bite into one and spit it out if you don't like it. Only I didn't realize I could do that.

In the back of my mind, I would frequently say commands like "Don't do this" or "Don't do that" to myself, followed with a long list of rules and roles I blindly emulated.

One day, when I was young, I was cautiously stirring my yogurt at lunch. I was being extremely mindful not to spill it over the edges. I wanted my parents to notice my efforts and approve of me. "Be a good girl and they will love you, " rang through my head. This phrase began an idealized view of life - Everything would be guaranteed to be good if I obeyed the authoritarian rules. I was so fearful of even the simple things not being accepted. I didn't even go outside the lines when I colored in my books.

My idealistic world view was severely punctured when I left home for college, where I learned no matter how "good" I tried to be, it was never enough. All the earlier preparations were about to fall away. Here I was, ready to make my mark on the world, feeling I had all the guidelines for success when unexpectedly, my parents divorced. I was devastated and sad. I felt abandoned and tapped into a well of grief I never knew existed. In addition to the sadness, an unwelcome message I came to understand well. "Even when you obey the rules, things can still fall apart." My primary foothold, my sure place to step from, was not shattered. I had nothing to replace my ideals, so I doubled down in the role as "good girl" and young adult.

Surrounding myself with people who generally believed as I did, was the key in attaining what my younger self still craved. You know, the sense of belonging, feeling like you mattered and loved. To remain in this state of "goodness" a part of me was positioned as a lookout. Always on alert to know what was needed or required. I found myself judging others to help me feel better about myself. Making these assessments didn't help as the patterns continued and would eventually blow up when I became a parent.

Unfortunately for me, the transition from the role of good girl to good mother wasn't working. Following my earlier internal commands of "Do this! Don't do that!" was not cutting it anymore. I couldn't magically cure the unexpected emotional outbursts. The feelings resulted in a world of frustration and confusion. Feeling overwhelmed came more frequently. When stressed, I would withdraw or numb the uncomfortable feelings with sugar, especially chocolate (Hershey's Kiss, anyone?). These emotions I was trying to stuff down inside hinted at something bigger going on. What could it be?

This is why I found myself in the chair at a therapist's office! Here I am, ready to rip off bows and tear through the shiny, pretty paper to get to the bottom of these mysterious presents! I needed to know and understand what it was my parents passed on to me. What were their "issues" and beliefs which made me feel so lost and frustrated as an adult? Like Forrest Gump, I was going through the boxes, one at a time, finding out what was there for me.

There were many things I would discover, "gifts" being a metaphor, of course. These were my boxes. Each one holding varying rules, responsibilities, and requirements for a well ordered and controlled life. It turns out, while they seemed unique in their wrappings, they were run of the mill gifts, passed along by my less than nurturing families, particularly members affected with functional addictions.

As I opened and looked inside the first box, I saw it was as dark as a starless night. "Is there even anything in here?" I wondered. I reached around and soon felt something cool to the touch. Out came a blind fold of midnight blue, so deep a blue it convinced you it was black. In the right light, however, it revealed a mesmerizing, blue shimmer. Voices emerged: "Don't trust your senses!" " There's no need to see for yourself." " Things aren't really a big deal unless everyone agrees they are." "Avoid feelings!"

To distract myself from the voices in my head, I reached around again. My fingers barely noticed a little stub of a paper, tucked away deep in a corner. A ticket to the movie, "Gaslight" (a classic with

Ingrid Bergman) appeared as I drew it into the light. In the film, a female character marries someone who wants to rob her blind. She is so convinced by her husband's perspective; she doubts her own version of reality. It comes to the point when it challenges her sanity. In order to save herself, she must rouse from her current reality and view what is really happening.

What a simple naïve perspective I had. I believed everything was fine in my family. We didn't talk about problems, especially the ones we lived with every day. When negative feelings arose, we simply found someone in the family to blame, a scapegoat. For the first time, the voices were being heard. They would bring me greater understanding eventually. Today, they speak loud and clear, especially when things aren't going so well. This level of change is called "awareness"! Perhaps you've experienced this, when you've had insight into a challenging situation, without the tools to change it. I wondered if therapy was going to reveal anything which could help heal and awaken me to a better journey in life.

The Ideal Woman was revealed in the second box , the one with the gorgeous wrapping in my imagination of course. After loosening the lid, an immense magazine with sticky notes and self-important reminder tabs popped out. A well thumbed and highlighted copy of "The Delightful, Dutiful Woman" magazine lay there in all its modest glory. Within its sacred pages, the cultural expectations of womanhood were clearly outlined, bullet-pointed and explained. Its messages perpetuated the notions of a proper, regimented and (supposedly) balance way of (external) life. Without realizing it, I had been one of its proud proponents, submitting to the never-ending list of demands. Constant bending over backwards, create healthy meals, always ready at a minute's notice, vacuum in one hand, a duster in the other hand, and the house must always be clean. Let's not forget the requirement of having beds made (fluff your throw pillows, anyone?) and clothes correctly folded and put away.

Along with all the above, is the community aspect. I should and must volunteer at the school and church. In spare time (even if none exists), locate anyone who may have a need and meet it by saying yes. Completing this perfect role will place one in a position of complete independence. There was no reason to develop self-introspection or time with all this busy-ness. I began to realize how frequently I sought the approval of others. Was I doing enough good? Did everyone agree with what or how I was doing something? Was the work up to their standards?

By now, I found myself exhausted. However, I spotted a smaller magazine, "The Ideal Daughter". As I examined it, a sudden realization jolted through my body. I saw my past and present collide, and a generational pattern of wounding emerge. Through a flash of insight, I connected how playing the role as the perfect child correlated with the current need to be the Ideal Woman. Shockingly, I discovered my experience as a child was largely based on how well I played the role of the perfect daughter. It made perfect to sense to me how I would perpetuate this same pattern in my role as parent. This became very painful for me and I felt powerless. What else could I do? Who am I supposed to be as a person and parent? I began to understand how expecting myself to perform a role, not have limits, not being able to say no was not humane to myself or my family. Believing one could perform their way through life is a big load of BS.

Now I could see how I was modeling this pattern to my own child. "I am superhuman (and you will be too)." I slowly became aware I had a choice about whether the opinions of others were more important than mine; especially when it came to what I believed of myself. I was finally able to say no and stick to it, even when the guilt arose in various degrees. I learned I had choices in my life! WOW! Imagine that?!

This reminded me of one of my favorite scenes in "Pride & Prejudice" (a beloved Jane Austen novel). Elizabeth Bennett refutes a proud person's interference in her personal life. She tells them she is resolved to make decisions for her own happiness, "without reference to you or any person so wholly unconnected with me." I could put people's opinion of me at a distance and not feel the need to correct or fix them. Even my closest loved ones don't have to agree with my reasons behind my choices. I have learned to be able to live with this idea.

After beginning the work of unearthing hidden messages from the boxes, I realized there was no going back. The crap was out, shaking things up in my world. Unsettling questions arose frequently. Big questions like "What is life and who am I?" I certainly couldn't make the wrapping look pretty anymore.

One afternoon, alone at home, I leaned over my kitchen table and began to sketch. A forlorn looking tree took shape, its branches snapped off.

Each branch represented something I thought I once knew but could no longer claim. Important things about life and relationships were labeled. I became aware of an unnamed fear, the part which wanted to control everything, that had been riding along with me in life. This fear had trapped the stories and messages from those boxes into my mind. To keep me safe, it had pressed them further into my body. This created incredible tension everywhere, especially in my neck, upper back and chest. At the bottom of the page, I was nudged to write, "What is Love?" I had no idea what the truest form of love might be. I sensed only intimations of it.

My hunched posture signaled long held self-protection. I was terrified of being vulnerable and having others identify my imperfections while still not having it all figured out. Thank God there was a week long program of intensive support for people facing these issues. And it was only an hour away! I packed my bags several months later in preparation to dig deeper into my boxes. For the first time to express feelings which had long been bottled up.

While participating in the program, the "nice girls don't get angry" box was ready to bust out of its well taped seams. I quickly reached into this one as it was jumping up and down. I expected a snake to pop out and strike! Instead, a soft floral silk cloth brushed my hand. It was a muted watercolor print; the right size to tie around your mouth and firmly knot behind your head. The messages spilled out in a sickly-sweet voice: "There's no reason to talk about feelings that aren't nice. " "Loyalty to family is of utmost importance." Stifling my negative emotions was second nature to me, as was protecting my loved ones. Ready to move beyond making excuses for another person's behavior, I stepped into a natural state of responding. As I tapped into the deep anger of not receiving what I needed as a child, I was supported to release it from my body. It was powerful! I WAS powerful! As the anger evaporated, I was able to go beyond it, touching the sadness buried below. Now the real work would begin. I was ready!

I was awakening. Perhaps you relate to feeling stuck and looking for a trap door to get out. The level of discomfort can be overwhelming. As I returned from digging around in almost ever corner of my gift boxes, I entered a dark night of the soul. I was not prepared for it; however, I would soon learn it was necessary.

There was much more to discover about myself and the healing which would bring me home to a place deep within me. During the week, I cracked open a door to peer at what I had long for, assurances of love and recognition telling me I was always enough just as I was. I had been introduced to my authentic self, my Inner Child, who has been who she is. All the gifts I received as a child had hidden this vital essence, the gift of myself, granted to me at birth. I am unique and original, with no need to change. I could be seen, heard, and connected. It turns out my inner child was my ticket to real life. "All is not as it seems" came the whisper. Up came feelings of anger, confusion and loneliness. I moved within a life that felt colorless and bland, my mind and body mired in difficult emotions. In some ways, I was in a worse place than when I had started a year ago. What the hell was healing anyway? This hurt worse than I wanted it to feel. The old pattern of repressing emotions, hard wired in my brain, was doing its best to deal with emotions no longer constrained. There were times I would find myself sitting on the couch staring out the window, trying to envision a world which made sense again. The deep, dark place of grief I wanted to disconnect and hide from continued for some time. Longer than I would have liked had I been able to dictate the healing process. I was still inside my boxes with these heavy feelings, and at the same time I was attempting to escape, trying for freedom. Grief can have a way of blinding you. While scrambling so hard to get out, I didn't realize grief WAS the ticket out. I was inching forward each time I allowed my feelings to come up and sit with them. I could sense my Inner Self, even if it were for a few minutes. Other times, flashes of bright light would shine through. I realized I had the ability to be aware in a challenging situation or choose to pause, allowing me a different way to respond. Ahhhh, I had a choice! I began to identify miscommunications and misunderstandings were a part of life. Even in a disagreement, sharing my thoughts and feelings could bring in the light of love into the situation. In turn, a deeper appreciation of the other person as an individual came about. I could be seen and more fully witness others.

One of the outcomes of this intensive work was a full-on rubber band stretched to its limits of emotional band width. Not only could I go and dive deeply into painful emotions, I could also go much further along the trajectory of joy and happiness. I could sense how my attempts to control life controlled me. I became aware how often we pile into spaces huddling together box to box, cold inside, not actually touching what is real. It's lonely living from a box. In order to heal and grow, I realized I need not be afraid of change. I must be connected to all the parts of myself, the ones I knew, didn't know, and sometimes didn't want to know. It was critical to find places and times where I could regularly open the doors of my inner world and share my realness with others. I required time without expectations from others. It was becoming clear to me in order to move forward, my go-to method of figuring things out in my mind was not going to grant me the peace I longed for. Perhaps sensing and feeling, versus thinking, could bring me something new?

In order to connect more deeply with myself, I started with healing my body and signed up for yoga classes. I did find being true to myself and my body was important in developing more self-acceptance. I stepped onto the mat and allowed my body to tell me things. Things like I wasn't a perfect yoga student (news flash! And yet we all are) and breathing while moving makes everything a whole lot easier. When my breath changes, it's a clue about something happening in my body. I continue to the tools as reminders to keep breathing by getting into a yoga pose or simply stretch my body. To be on the mat and just feel, helps me to connect deeper.

In time, the need for deep grieving lightened. My feet landed softly in a place of understanding and acceptance of myself. There was an internal expansiveness, an invitation to lightness and movement. My Inner Child had assisted me in feeling and was willing to guide me to what made me happy, what made me ME. I was seeking an invisible gift I had possessed since birth. I opened to using expressive art as a healing process. I found by welcoming the parts of myself which were easily excluded from daily life was extremely important. The parts which don't have a productive purpose according to a society hell-bent on action. The beauty was, I didn't have to be an official artist to get these gifts – I just had to show up as myself and be willing to do whatever came next.

I feel deeply connecting with others is the ultimate way to live. Fostering authentic connections with others in a safe space is the ultimate guide to finding a life we love and a life full of meaning. My happiest moments are connecting and witnessing others as they connect themselves in whatever form they are engaged in, whether it's writing, yoga or expressive arts. These spaces hold room for our hearts and souls. We can show our inner selves and learn more about what makes us the same and different from one another. Celebrating our uniqueness is sadly lacking in our culture.

I have learned to sit in and create safe spaces, honoring creative voices of others as well as my own; a place to speak and be heard. What would the world feel and look like if more of us were willing to experiment with dropping the boxes of a preconceived life and truly sense ourselves in the moment, breath by breath as we move to create? Are we willing to learn we need to include our imperfections, uniqueness within our being? Letting our bodies lead us in dance our paint brushes or pens to create a new vista on the blank page before us, allows for a fresh energy to emerge.

I have learned using art as a process creates opportunity for the deep healing of ourselves. In the middle of my therapy, when I started to sense of this shifting, I knew my life was now a canvas and I could express myself. I allow myself to be present now, in any experience which arises. Each time I dip my brush in the paint, I release judgement. Working with the 'ugly' spaces on the canvas is simply holding a space for the 'ugly' spaces I think are within me. The old stories I tell myself can shift as I engage differently with them on canvas. I can watch them unfold or try to stop, judge, and control them. I have the choice of simply letting them be as the painting continues to unfold, stroke by stroke.

My mind becomes engaged with the process, versus trying to judge and control it. By following a non-linear path, my intuition – where my soul/inner self is guiding me, I am free to boldly express myself; always changing, no need for perfection, flowing with energy and love. Will I dance outside the box or hide is always the question?

What lies beyond your current understanding or experience? That is the mystery which unfolds as you drop the rules and allow your creative, intuitive self to lead the way. This part of us celebrates in such opportunities and can be reawakened.

Although I wish life had been handed to me in a neat little package with a pretty bow on top, containing only loving words and healthy beliefs, the presents I received gave me many things. It is the gift to be able to discern, to have the option to live life more authentically, to feel and fearlessly express all my emotions, and to connect with myself. This includes all my imperfections and uniqueness. I have learned to feel and appreciate fear and vulnerability. With each deep breath, I take in the newness of life, while being led by my heart and soul. I take a step along an unseen path, with no guarantee except freedom, love, and a deep belonging to a unique, created self and all which exists within that love is everything.

I am learning to lean into a sense of enough-ness. Beyond my limited world view is one so expansive, extending an invitation for each of us! We are all welcomed to participate beyond the conditioning of our cultures and family systems. You won't be surprised to know I was terrified of the dark as a kid. It seemed the worse possible experience I could have as a child. Now I have opened the door and wonder what adventures will come? What further healing lays in store?

I have found my expressive arts practice to be a bridge between the parts of me which try to be informed by the old box rules and the open, free parts which follows the whisper of " all is not as it seems".

Looking into the night sky tonight, the clouds pass by and reveal the north star and a bright planet. There is so much more I want to explore, to open myself to the next space, releasing the broken down (and recycled!) boxes behind me.

As I write, I am sitting on the living room couch. I am feeling whole, and more complete with a greater understanding. That is a true gift!

"Now all the glory of God, who is able, through his mighty power at work within us, to accomplish infinitely more than we might ask or think. Glory to him in the church and in Christ Jesus through all generations forever and ever. Amen"

Ephesians 3:20-21

As a business development professional and sales manager in highly competitive industries for more than 35 years, Maureen brings a uniquely creative breadth and depth of experience, as well as strategy, to her life coaching practice.

Her passion for inspiring people to new levels, breaking through paradigms for transformative growth, and encouraging true gifts and purpose to shine have enabled her employees and clients to excel beyond expectation. A renewed joy, happiness, creativity, passion and connection results along with richer more authentic relationships with themselves and others. She is a humble, compassionate soul who holds in high regards the opportunity to partner with people in ways that enable them to have a life they absolutely love.

Maureen enjoys relaxing and refueling with long walks barefoot along the Sarasota shores, meditating in nature, listening to inspirational music and reading inspirational scripture and books such as this one. Her favorite time is spent in the company of loving friends and family who inspire her to be a better version of herself with every passing day. She can also be found on occasion with a paint brush in hand or an artist's journal on her lap sketching visions that inspire her in the moment. She's a daughter, sister, friend, mother, and business partner just like you, who desires to leave a legacy of loving kindness.

Website: www.BeyondBlessed4Life.com
Email: Maureen@BeyondBlessed4Life.com
mlimpact@yahoo.com

MAUREEN
HATFIELD

Life Coach, Business Development
Professional, Sales Manager

To souls who's hearts are ready to journey into a new
realm of delicious authentic relationship.
To my friends who inspired me to live brilliantly bold.
To the one who unlocked my heart to experience pure love.

When God
Shows Up

Insanity? As I sit in front of my computer, no sleep, exhausted, thinking my life is put together well, I feel so undone. I have come to the realization there is no more of 'me'. Who am I anyway? I have been ripped in so many different directions. Pieces of me scattered across the floor like a dish that broke into a millions pieces, almost impossible to pick them all up.

My life feels impossible, overwhelming, I'm grieving. Is it the loss of a marriage or am I grieving the loss of myself. I chose to give and take care of everything and everyone. How can I blame anyone now?

Tears roll down my face, anger rages inside and all I want to do is run away from everyone and everything to a secluded island, where no one can reach me. If only I can shut the world out, even if for a few days, how wonderful that could feel. How can I be a 'supermom', or a sales manager for my team pulling top performing numbers, when I am such a hot mess? God please help me.

God was about to help in a way I had never imagined. Somehow He felt it was time for me to write my story and everything aligned. His mighty power would surely be at work. I had no idea until this day. My appointment was scheduled with my writing coach. I didn't even want to take the call with her. I was at the end of myself questioning everything. I found myself stuck, unable to write or edit anything. I just couldn't do it. How could I face her and tell her I let another week slip by, always making excuses. Cancel, I thought. It won't matter, right?

I didn't want my imperfections to be found out. Would she see them? Would she know? After all, she's a coach. She know things. I couldn't let her know I have masks I hide behind, it was too real and raw for me. Right before I got on the phone, I had to shake it off – I could not concentrate – my head was swirling – I couldn't even put a sentence together – there was so much chaos. I was pacing between the kitchen and the bathroom. I looked like hell and wanted desperately to cover it all up with foundation, eye liner and mascara and pop some fun color lipstick to tie myself all up in a pretty package before being on the camera. In the kitchen was my pot of coffee – one cup, then a second and onto my third - attempting to wake myself up and clear the storm raging in my mind. OMG, what is she going to think of me?

Then it hit me - PERFECTIONISM – it wreaks absolute havoc and has never served me! Yet again, I was trying to put on all these facades and make life look like it's all nip tucked and buttoned up. Tuck? Just tuck me back under the covers and let me sleep.

Somehow I knew talking with her would be good. My mind rushed through a thousand thoughts. Things like, "People want that all together, got it all under control kind of gal in their lives." I knew they really wanted true connection.

Off came my mask and down came the wall. If I wasn't going to be honest then I would continue the same way in life and keep people away from my heart, like Fort Knox. I wonder if we are all trying so hard to make our lives look a certain way, rather than simply being true and authentic to ourselves and others?

A true authentic journey where transformation and healing takes place, where I can find the richness of life and passion happening. That's what I decided I wanted. That's where people find themselves – whole and complete! The place where I can not only just breathe again, but start to dance, sing, paint and want to be with people, sharing intimately, deeply rich. It opens up the world at a whole new level. Just by being in my own physical presence in that honest place, hot mess and all, the good, bad and ugly, I was going to accept myself. That was what was missing.

That's when God showed up, my lifeline, and right on time as always! He hit me with spiritual 2x4's to wake me up. Then He revealed to me who I really am. I am His beloved daughter who is more than enough in His eyes! There is nothing I must do to be loved by Him. He knows what He must do to reach me and deal with me. As I'm pouring myself out into everyone and every situation in my path, He stops me dead in my tracks. Reminding me that even as a Life Coach ... these patterns of overachiever perfectionism still exist. They are running the show again even though I thought I was past all this.

Laughing at myself as a thought pops into my mind: ' Was I divorcing myself from a husband? The truth is, I'm divorcing myself from myself and my own insanity'!

The insanity of this belief, that somehow I am not enough, and I'll never be enough. A 'lack mentality' as if there is not enough time, not enough money, and certainly not enough of me! Then I have a real awakening. OMG, that's why I attract narcissists! I attract narcissistic relationships, and have for most of my life, because I must ultimately prove my worth and value to feed my own ego. The part of my ego that craves to be enough in order to feel okay. That part of my 'empathic giver' personality that must feed the 'absolute taker' personality. Now if that's not insanity, then I don't know what is? Wait a minute, who is taking from whom? Slapping my hand on my forehead another enlightening moment hit me.

As I'm stopped and confronted by these massive 2x4 blows, I begin to reflect from a fresh perspective. How did I get here? Where did I ever adopt this belief of not being enough? Digging deeper, peeling the layers of the onion. When did I actually allow God in – really in – into the depth of my soul? How did I do it, because now I need to do that in the rest of my life? I didn't really know God intimately until I needed Him most, in my ugliest moment, when my world came crashing down all around me. Was I only using God for my own gain?

How could it all fall apart so quickly? Why did I have to lose my six-figure job, have my marriage fall apart and alienate myself from most of my friends? All to hide the real me and the relentless pain of failure.

Prior to that moment my relationship with God was not authentic, it was intellectual at best. I'll never forget sitting at my kitchen table, sipping tea with my dearest friend, having a profound conversation about God - a saving God, a 'real living God', not just from scripture and in a faraway untouchable place. She was sharing how God sees us as our biological father would, not just our heavenly one. We are physically His biological kids, oh wow, just like my earthly father. My dad would lay His life down for me. The epiphany hit, I realized and started to understand my relationship with God in a completely different light. He is right here, right now, and views me as an actual crown jewel daughter. All of a sudden, I let pure unconditional love pour into my system, probably for the first time, and I wept uncontrollably from the emotion of it. A joy that pure love brings, which I had never really known before, filled me. The release of stress, overwhelm, depression and trying to be something you are not tangibly melts away. I felt embraced by my Loving God and relaxed into his arms.

Yet, what is showing up in my life now is actually because of it all – my willingness to dive deep into my healing and be vulnerable, messy, and bolder than ever before. These were the stepping stones upon which I can get to that next level in my life. That level where sheer joy resides, I wanted it! In fact, sharing so genuinely with people – allowing them in to see that big mess on the floor called 'ME' – is exactly what's healing everyone around me! It's crazy! It's contagious!

It's true what you put up is a ripple effect and it's unleashing peoples' inner child at magnitudes and levels rarely experienced. The walls start to come crashing down. It frees us from the bondage of lies and inauthentic ways of being that have held us down. I find myself constantly reaching through my own stuff, getting out of my comfort zones and I've been cracked open like a bee's hive! Not only does it take me out of my own comfort zones, people are sharing with me how blown away they are at the extent to which I will go to help them and save themselves in the middle of my own raging battles! Is it true if we love another neighbor as we love ourselves we are a living commandment?

I was able to start the process of taking down the veils of looking a particular way for God, taking the masks off, to just be real with him, even though he already knew me better than I knew myself. I imagined him sitting right next to me, like I would do with my dad, placing my head in his lap as all the cares of my world melted away … and there was no more of me. The more I spend time imagining this, the easier and more tangible it becomes. I can choose to put myself in this visual space with God, instantly now. I have been taking the journey to "come to Him." I have a visual of him sitting on a massive rock by the side of a beautiful stream where I typically kneel on the ground with my head at His feet in gratitude and exhaustion. It feels lifelike, like a real relationship now. I don't have to ask a certain way, my conversation doesn't have to look a certain way, I don't have to be perfect any longer. I am 100% forgiven in all my mess. I found my true self, and I can just simply be myself here. Unconditionally accepted.

Ironically, this new found relationship with God and myself enables me to step into my bolder truer voice, sharing in unique ways that help clients unlock and unfold themselves. It heals! OMG, that's it! I can genuinely choose to love myself and others from that genuine space. In that choice comes a compassion and openness that surpasses rational thought. It enables conversations that create breakthrough moments, viewing life itself from new vantage points.

So, where did this all start, this 'I am not enough' conversation? Sipping my cup of tea with all these revelations circulating, wondering where all this insanity began, memories of my parents rang through my head. Statements that echoed through our home growing up. A generational belief held onto tightly... "Let people see your strength not weakness." "Never let people see that side, the messy one." "Those skeletons are meant to be kept in the closet." "Don't air your dirty laundry." "Zip your lip so you don't burden people with your problems." These beliefs color our world and cost us love, intimacy, health, joy, celebration and create the chasm between the facades so you don't have access to your own undisputed truth. You are always told "DON'T SHOW IT." How can any of us ever be authentic under the weight of that belief?

There's a general misconception in our culture

that people will view you as weak, take advantage of you, walk all over you, won't be around you if you show vulnerability. People are not interested in that ugly, shadow side. The truth is, however, being inauthentic keeps you from connecting with people at a juicer level, that really rich and amazing part of life, rather we chose to sacrifice it to only at a superficial layer. The truth is, there is real power and strength in that vulnerability, it opens the realm of unconditional love and pure intimate relationship, to self and others.

I'm discovering also that I am deeply empathetic. I actually feel people, their emotions, their physical pains as well as their happiness and joy. I have an uncanny ability to sense energy levels within individuals and even groups – HIGHS & LOWS. I can walk into a crowded environment like NYC, where I worked for years, and literally feel what people are feeling around me – happiness – joy – sadness – loneliness – victory – failure – love – anger – frustration - all of it. People comment often that I can read their minds or ask how I knew that about them when I barely know them. I can feel the needs so intensely, I can give and pour back into many exactly what they need at a moment's notice ... the ultimate giver personality. No wonder I am exhausted and out of touch with my own feelings. My caretaker empath side did not have a clue who she really was, nor what her value was. I am the girl who looks like she has it all together on the outside - which is why everyone comes to me - like the rock who cannot be chiseled nor broken. But what this really covered up was how I really felt deep down inside … like I was never enough – like I'll never be worthy to be accepted or valued or even loved!

Imagine having this driving force underneath the ultimate giver-performer personality … just imagine it for a minute … or maybe you even recognize it … maybe this is you too? Or maybe you know someone close to you who is similar. It's exhausting and can debilitate you, stealing your health, intimacy and happiness if you're not careful. It is subtle when it comes to rob you. By the time you recognize it, you are completely drained. You are already physically and emotionally debilitated. Health symptoms can show up as adrenal fatigue, severe depression or so many other diagnosable things. This set of characteristics is sometimes a deadly combination but on the other side it is such a highly satisfying and life sustaining force – a blessing - to be able to help and serve people in such impactful ways. I've had people come back to me and share that I stopped them from suicidal attempts, saved some marriages, and helped some be able to walk away from relationships or careers that were not healthy for them. Was I helping, filling my ego or both? The mere fact I feed on helping them, is it a good thing or am I lost in an abyss of feeding my own insecurity?

I realize I have another characteristic that takes over, my insatiable nature. I can never get enough of anything. I always have to have more or do more or be more. Not only am I not good enough – I can't get enough! Complete insanity! It's like an addiction. I am the insatiable overachieving perfectionist. The gal who delivers 200% all the time, in a world surrounded by rather large, fragile egos with highly narcissistic tendencies. People that can literally suck the life energy right out of you like a vampire. I thought it was only present in my personal relationship, but as I look back on my life, it has been there for so much longer, in friendships, in career and community relationships, as well as my intimate realm. In order to heal I had to keep looking in the mirror and ask, "What is it about ME, not them, ME? What did I need that attracts this 'NARCISSITIC' personality like a high-powered magnet?" I was obviously being served in some way too.

By definition, narcissism is a mental condition in which people have an inflated sense of their own importance, a deep need for excessive attention and admiration and a lack of empathy for others ... it's the pursuit of gratification from vanity or egotistic admiration of one's idealized self-image including self-flattery, perfectionism, and arrogance. A narcissist uses other people solely for their own wants, needs and gratification. They use highly seductive and manipulative techniques to lure you into their web like a black widow spider. Once you recognize that you have lost yourself and want to regain your own identity the narcissist begins to devalue you ferociously as a coping mechanism to turn the attention back onto themselves always ... a gigantic and ugly cat and mouse game.

As I look deeper and deeper into the mirror, peeling back layers of the onion called ME, I realize that my world is about to be forever changed. Like a jeweler investigates all the facets of a diamond, I begin to see all the different elements of narcissism in my life and it's affects. Why was I involved in a relationship for so many years where I felt like I had to be perfect all the time? Why did I desire and need such gratification to be noticed, to be perfect, to be loved? I was walking on eggshells, caught in a conundrum of giving and yet feeling like I was being punished. I could never make a mistake. If I did, conflict would arise, bringing with it a wrath that punished nonstop. It was debilitating, making me feel like curling up and withering way. My beautiful spirit, my inner child would die a slow grueling death. A raging battle of emotions, like gale force winds and baseball-size hail hitting me from all directions, with no reprieve. Its name is Narcissism!

It sucks the very life right out of you ,moment by moment, until you look into the mirror and don't even recognize the image staring back at you. How does this 'strong sense of self' woman even begin to fall prey to such an ordeal? Well, it's simple. The narcissist wears cleverly designed masks to lure even the wisest of wise into their seductive web. While easy to play the blame game here, I had to look at my role in the matter! My ego needed to be fed at that level! YES! My ego! What? I needed to feel whole and complete. I needed to pour that much of me, my attention, my value, my everything into the bottomless cavern of someone else who desired all the attention. It fed my need to prove I was enough! It fed my insatiable side! It fed that piece of my perfectionistic ego because I needed to be perfect to keep the peace in my home. But the truth was – it was all a façade too! Oh, the walls come tumbling down!

How the hell do I heal from this? And God shows up again, although the reality is He never left. Unconditional love and acceptance, He reminds me as I see His face when I close my eyes to the chaos. Simply choose! Choose to love myself again as He has loved me. Choose to forgive myself as He has forgiven me. Choose to accept myself inside of it all – the good, the bad and the ugly. Choose to quiet the chaos and storms and walk out in faith. Choose to bring joy and happiness back in because this is a sustaining life force. Exercise the power of choice!

So, there it is. Choose to divorce myself from the insanity – literally sign a piece of paper as if going to court to dissolve a marriage. As I begin this process of choosing to love myself and accept myself in all of it, I fill myself back up differently. It's like reinventing myself and investigating the things that bring me joy and happiness, such as listening to inspirational music when I wake up, dancing around the house in the middle of the day, taking time with friends to celebrate life. Even sweet fulfilling walks on the beach to fill my soul back up are healing. I run to the nearby Hobby Lobby, a craft store and purchase a brand new journal and set of over 20 colors of pens, open it to the first page and begin a new chapter! I start to breathe again, letting it all in! My first couple of pages fill with the things that bring me joy. I start to take my life back. Love floods back in as my true and authentic self takes over with God's grace. My inner child awakes stretching her arms up toward the sun to shine again! I had no idea when I began to tell my story, that the healing I truly needed would unfold. It began so differently, full of blame and now the layers revealed exactly what God wanted me to see.

Then God showed up again and brought a loving relationship into my life to test my love on many levels. How can I possibly be in any type of relationship, when I am like this? Who would have ever imagined that out of this very insanity, the more I share the real me in a new relationship with a man that I adore, the deeper he falls into pure unconditional love! It breaks every rational belief system I've ever held tightly onto. He tells me in so many ways that he's in love with me, that he has never met someone who talks so openly and authentically sweet. Nobody loves so big and bold and so easily and more genuinely compassionate. He tells me all the time that I am so easy to love. Even with all this mess that is going on in my life!

How could that even be possible?

The divine timing of this process changed my entire perspective. When we choose responsibility over shame, blame and guilt we awaken to the real truth of our lives and our role in it all. The mirror was held in front of me when I first began this process, it wasn't easy by any means having my writing coach show me the other side. Boy, that was a wake up call and it's exactly how I help others see the truth. It made perfect sense looking back upon this process.

God, you are truly funny bringing this into my life, to be raw and strip away the masks I was wearing, so I can really see who I am and who I want to become. God, you showed up in a way I never saw coming, even while I was angry, complaining and blaming in an unhealthy relationship, when actually it was all a choice. I made a choice to reconnect with the infinite and divine love of greatness, to open my heart in a new way, which I'm still learning and to receive the kind of love I so often give to others. I had to show up too, Thank you God. You showed up in more ways I may have ever imagined. I pray that others in the world come to know you as I have.

"Our deepest fear is not that we are inadequate. Our deepest fear is that we are powerful beyond measure. It is our light, not our darkness that most frightens us."

- Marianne Williamson

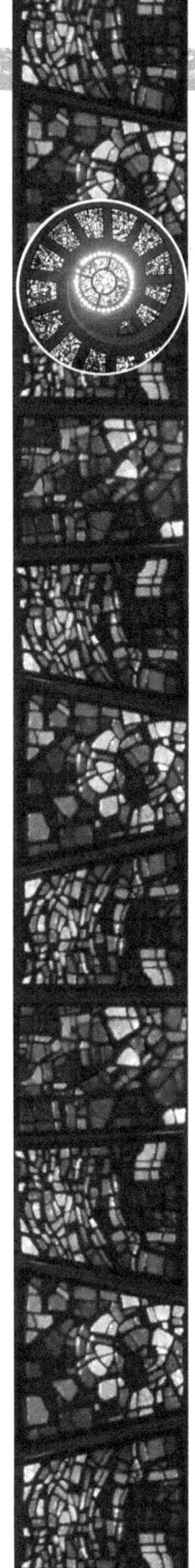

Conclusion

Candy Lyn Thomen
Artist, Graphic Designer

The clouds outside my window raced by, driven by the cold, early spring winds. March was going to go out like a lion this year. Sitting at home in my art studio thinking about my mom, I felt so lost in this vast unknown of life without her. Her sudden death eight months before had brought large parts of my life crashing down around me. Eight months and I was no closer to having any answers about who I was and what I was supposed to do now, than I did when she disappeared from my world. Amid the emotional chaos in my mind, I began thinking about why I found

myself in this place of starting over yet again. Why did I keep coming back to this point?

There had been many times I experienced a significant loss or change in my life. In the depths of the transformation, during those deep, dark times before the rebuilding starts, I always felt like I was on a cruel wheel, turning around and around, bringing me back to the same damn spot in my life. "Why can't I ever get past this place?" I would cry, feeling completely sorry for myself. I didn't comprehend this continuous cycle of death and rebirth bringing me back to lessons I still needed to learn.

This pattern had repeated too many times in my life, between divorce, family and business shake-ups. There comes a time when certain patterns keep repeating, when we must finally stop, look inside and ask the question, "Do I truly want to heal?" On the surface, everyone always answers, "Yes, of course I want to heal!" Who really wants to look inside and hear their own voice say, "NO! I don't want to heal. I want to stay stuck, right here where I'm at and blame everything I am 'going through' on someone or something else." This was where I was at today. The time had come for me to make a decision. Did I want to heal myself? Was I willing to do what was being asked of me by the Universe, to honor who I truly am? "Who is that?" I ask.

A friend of mine has this beautiful floral brooch created from small pieces of broken glass. She talks about how the pieces of glass are like our lives, and the mosaic is how we put the pieces together to make something new and beautiful. How often had I trod on the pieces of previous parts of my life without looking at the beauty contained within them?

Rarely had I stopped to appreciate the beauty of the new life I was creating from the shattered pieces of my past, clinging instead to what the pieces used to look like, what they used to represent. Instead of embracing the magnificence of what existed now, I would only mourn the loss.

The more significant aspect to life altering events is observing the changes and growth that happen within me each time I go through the process. Not only am I creating a new life, I am growing into a more awakened, higher-conscious version of myself. The one who recently began looking at all of my past experiences and appreciating them for what they truly were; stepping stones to this place of awareness. Each "tragedy" or life crisis actually pushed me forward to be the person I am right now, which is exactly who I need to be at the time I need to be it.

The most valuable part of walking the path of awakening is the ability to step back and step out of victim-mode, to begin to see life as a vast library of higher spiritual learning instead of a hamster-wheel of pain and suffering.

When I started on my path of awakening, it was on the island of Kauai, Hawaii, studying an ancient Hawaiian spiritual and healing way of life called Lomilomi. While I had always known there was something "more" to the Universe and my part in it, the path truly started at this point in my life. There were so many messages and symbols I received while on this retreat. Daily, symbols like crabs (forward motion but in a sideways dance not a straight line,) waves (representing our emotions and the constant rise and fall of life), spiders (story tellers and the web of life) would show up. All representing the various paths of spiritual awakening and how it plays out for us individually. I learned the signs are always present, the messages are always there, simply waiting for us to connect to our center and higher source in order to see and hear them.

I had been introduced to meditation not too long before all of this. After my time on Kauai, it became a tool I used daily to connect with my inner self and the greater spiritual world around me. During meditation I slowly flow inward, which then allows me to flow outward. I did not realize at the time, this flowing energy is the path of a spiral. For me, meditation is the practice of quieting my mind so I can actively listen to God, the natural and spiritual world, aligning myself to the more subtle messages of spirit and nature that surround me but are hard to hear in the static of our everyday world.

When I am still and make this connection to the energy that surrounds all that is, I am filled with overpowering love and gratitude. In this space of love and gratitude, my heart is filled to overflowing, my questions are answered, and all is right in my inner Universe.

When you are on a path of spiritual development and awakening, you are in the spiral. The nature of a spiral moves energy and awareness downward and upward, inward and outward. When you are awakening, you do both at the same time, moving inward as you expand outward, spiraling into your center while your awareness grows and moves outward, always building the new on what went before.

The spiral is an ancient, sacred symbol that represents the journey and change of life as it unfolds. The symbolism of this journey can be experienced by taking a walk in a labyrinth. (A labyrinth is a singular path that leads to a center, often in a circular shape. They are an ancient archetype dating back 4,000 years or more, used symbolically, as a walking meditation, choreographed dance, or site of rituals and ceremony, among other things.)

The spiral symbol can represent the consciousness of nature, beginning from its center expanding outwards. Spirals have been linked to nature, the seasons, and the path of life: birth, growth, death and reincarnation. The spiral is one of the oldest geometric shapes found throughout the ancient world. It is fundamental to nature, appearing in animals such as snails, seashells, and occurring in natural phenomena of whirlpools, hurricanes, tornadoes and spinning galaxies. The spiral has become a powerful symbol for creation and growth, used by many ancient cultures and religious traditions.

The motion of the spiral reminds me that we too, are always in motion, albeit rarely in the straight line we think we need or want. When I gaze up at the stars and the Milky way, I am in awe of our galaxy, along with the countless other stars and galaxies in our Universe. They grow outward as they spin, expanding, growing brighter. Their spinning motion starts more stardust to swirling, and those spirals grow and become new galaxies, a miraculous dance of the cosmos.

Mandalas offer the same energy as spirals, drawing you in towards the center and then bringing you back out again. Mandala is Sanskrit for "circle" and is a geometric design that holds a great deal of symbolism. Mandalas are said to be vessels that are used to bring us closer to God. The belief is by entering the mandala, either by creating one or meditating upon one, and proceeding towards its center, you are guided through the cosmic process of transforming the universe from one of suffering into one of joy and happiness. Meant to represent wholeness and a model for the organizational structure of life itself, a mandala is a cosmic diagram showing the relation to the infinite and the world which extends beyond and within minds and bodies.

I began channeling and drawing mandalas several years ago. Spirals are incorporated into many of them. They are a reminder that I need to go ever further into my own center in order to grow and move forward, to expand, to become more truly who I am meant to be. The energy contained in the mandalas is powerful and healing.

Over the course of the past ten years, I have learned while I may return to circumstances or lessons that feel all too familiar and painful, I always come back on a higher level than where I was before. This I learned from the magic of the spiral. It is impossible to ever return to exactly the same place I've been before, regardless of how much I try to feel otherwise about it. Holding greater knowledge and understanding, there are miles of difference between where I was even a year ago and where I find myself now. I have learned so much along the way; new perspectives, new ways of thinking and being, older, wiser, more mature, with different people supporting and nurturing me. This is how we learn, how we grow.

Truly, we are all spiritual beings experiencing this world in a human shell. We are the avatar of our own lives, constantly changing, growing, learning, BE-ing. Our worth is undefinable; and certainly not defined by what we DO. It is who we are. This journey of becoming, of awakening, some may think it has an end, a destination we arrive at. Once there, everything is magically okay, perfect, wonderful. I have learned time and again it is not a destination. The path of awakening is the journey. It never stops, never ends. We are always on the path. Even when we become frustrated and angry, even when we think we're done with it and step off, thinking never to return. Our innermost being, will always desire to continue the journey forward, because that is who and what we are.

Grateful for my years of spiritual study and practice, I now understand this journey is not circular, bringing me back to the same place over and over again like I used to think. It is a beautiful mosaic of learning and experience which has led me to exactly where I am at right now, to become exactly who I need to be in this moment. To grow and keep on expanding.

Through my process of awakening I have come to see and know my shadow self and am learning to integrate it so I can be more of who I am meant to be. The universe is made of energy. Energy surrounds us in all things, at all times. When we open to receive it, the energy of Source supports us and connects us to all living things. We are never, ever alone. Creating is one of the quickest ways to connect to God/ Source. We are all creators and the Universe wants to create through us. In my deepest, darkest turmoil the simple act of cooking a meal or picking up a pen to write or draw will open the creative channel and allow the love of God to flow into me and through me, healing what is out of alignment. Just as water can be so many things, when we flow with love and gratitude, life just simply gets better.

If I have anything to offer about this path of awakening, it would be this: Gratitude and love are the two surest ways to achieve any level of insight, and enlightenment. When I silence the voices in my mind, and listen to the voice of my heart, my path becomes far clearer and the emotional pain I sometimes struggle with dissipates. Meditation, prayer, and creating are all ways I use to quiet the brain/ego chatter and allow my spirit and heart to expand. When my heart expands, love flows, beauty abounds, I am connected with life and the universe, healing is so much easier and I am willing to step out and help those who want and need it. Because of my path of spiritual awakening, I feel the presence of my mom surrounding me; her love is always with me.

Each story in this book has been both a beautiful mosaic and a spiral. The shattered pieces of life are remade into authentic, genuine works of art. The path of awakening, spiraling inward and outward, into the center of who each person truly is and back out again, enabling each person to give their authentic, cherished gifts to themselves and the world.

I invite you now, at whatever point you're at in your life, to pause and go inward. Seek the beautiful pieces of your own mosaic, bring them into the light so you can see just how beautiful you are, inside and out.

Let the magic of the spiral carry you upward with inspiration and joy as you draw in the energy and love of God and the Universe. Remember wherever you're at in your own journey of awakening, you will have so much more wisdom and higher perspective. To learn more, to share more, to become more whole as the spiral lifts you once again, creating your own mosaic of love.

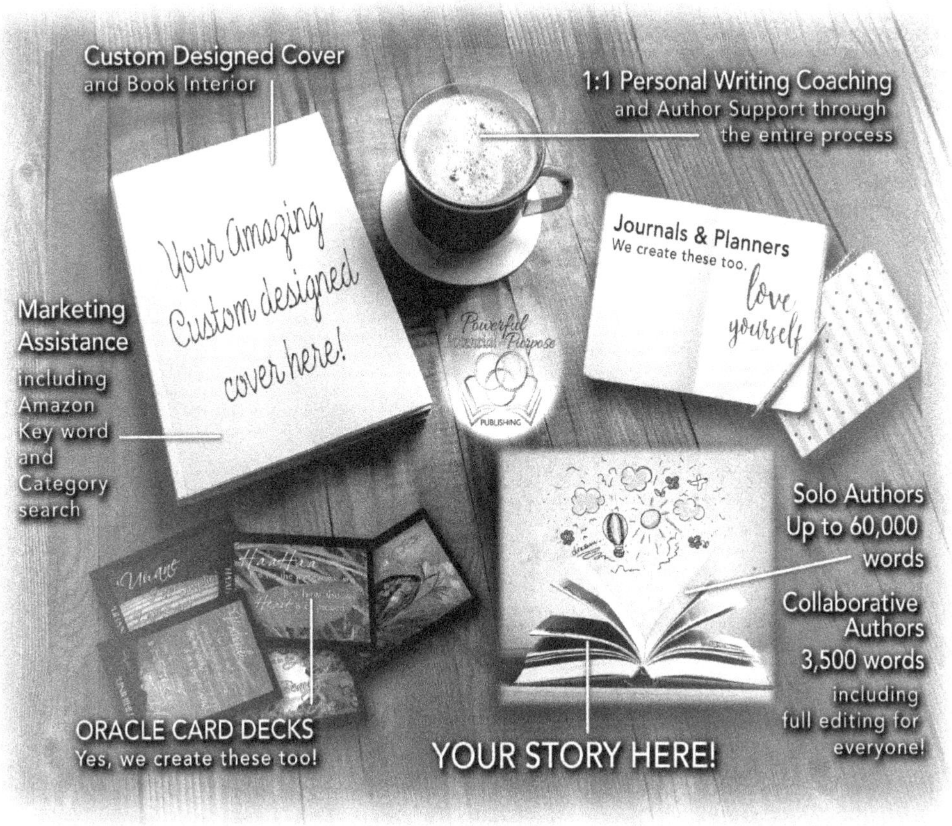

Custom Designed Cover
and Book Interior

1:1 Personal Writing Coaching
and Author Support through
the entire process

Your Amazing
Custom designed
cover here!

Journals & Planners
We create these too.

love
yourself

Marketing
Assistance
including
Amazon
Key word
and
Category
search

Solo Authors
Up to 60,000
words

Collaborative
Authors
3,500 words
including
full editing for
everyone!

ORACLE CARD DECKS
Yes, we create these too!

YOUR STORY HERE!

Gloria Coppola
Visionary, Author, Inspirational Speaker, Spiritual Minister
Publisher, Creative Writing Coach

My journey has lead me to my soul purpose, helping others heal and reaching their potential. As a natural intuitive my gifts bring your dreams alive and tap into the essence of your soul wisdom. Together, we raise the consciousness on this planet.

Candy Lyn Thomen
Intuitive Artist and Graphic Designer, Creative "Maker"
I love helping people bring their vision to life. Through my gifts as an intuitive and empath, I am able to connect with your vision and your energy to create a design that embodies your dream and is something you LOVE!

Powerful
Potential and Purpose

www.PPP-Publishing.com
828-713-3521
gloria@gloriacoppola.com

PUBLISHING

Made in USA - North Chelmsford, MA
1096928_9781734965506
05.01.2020 1554